Neo4j High Performance

Design, build, and administer scalable graph database
systems for your applications using Neo4j

Sonal Raj

BIRMINGHAM - MUMBAI

Neo4j High Performance

First published: February 2015

Production reference: 1250215

Published by Packt Publishing Ltd.
Livery Place
35 Livery Street
Birmingham B3 2PB, UK.

ISBN 978-1-78355-515-4

www.packtpub.com

Credits

Author
Sonal Raj

Reviewers
Roar Flolo
Dave Meehan
Kailash Nadh

Commissioning Editor
Kunal Parikh

Acquisition Editor
Shaon Basu

Content Development Editor
Akshay Nair

Technical Editor
Faisal Siddiqui

Copy Editors
Deepa Nambiar
Ashwati Thampi

Project Coordinator
Mary Alex

Proofreaders
Simran Bhogal
Maria Gould
Ameesha Green
Kevin McGowan
Jonathan Todd

Indexer
Hemangini Bari

Graphics
Abhinash Sahu
Valentina Dsilva

Production Coordinator
Alwin Roy

Cover Work
Alwin Roy

About the Author

Sonal Raj is a hacker, Pythonista, big data believer, and a technology dreamer. He has a passion for design and is an artist at heart. He blogs about technology, design, and gadgets at `http://www.sonalraj.com/`. When not working on projects, he can be found traveling, stargazing, or reading.

He has pursued engineering in computer science and loves to work on community projects. He has been a research fellow at SERC, IISc, Bangalore, and taken up projects on graph computations using Neo4j and Storm. Sonal has been a speaker at PyCon India and local meetups on Neo4j and has also published articles and research papers in leading magazines and international journals. He has contributed to several open source projects.

Presently, Sonal works at Goldman Sachs. Prior to this, he worked at Sigmoid Analytics, a start-up where he was actively involved in the development of machine learning frameworks, NoSQL databases, including Mongo DB and streaming using technologies such as Apache Spark.

I would like to thank my family for encouraging me, supporting my decisions, and always being there for me. I heartily want to thank all my friends who have always respected my passion for being part of open source projects and communities while reminding me that there is more to life than lines of code. Beyond this, I would like to thank the folks at Neo Technologies for the amazing product that can store the world in a graph. Special thanks to my colleagues for helping me validate my writings and finally the reviewers and editors at Packt Publishing without whose efforts this work would not have been possible. Merci à vous.

About the Reviewers

Roar Flolo has been developing software since 1993 when he got his first job developing video games at Funcom in Oslo, Norway. His career in video games brought him to Boston and Huntington Beach, California, where he cofounded Papaya Studio, an independent game development studio. He has worked on real-time networking, data streaming, multithreading, physics and vehicle simulations, AI, 2D and 3D graphics, and everything else that makes a game tick.

For the last 10 years, Roar has been working as a software consultant at www.flologroup.com, working on games and web and mobile apps. Recent projects include augmented reality apps and social apps for Android and iOS using the Neo4j graph database at the backend.

Dave Meehan has been working in information technology for over 15 years. His areas of specialty include website development, database administration, and security.

Kailash Nadh has been a hobbyist and professional developer for over 13 years. He has a special interest in web development, and is also a researcher with a PhD in artificial intelligence and computational linguistics.

www.PacktPub.com

Support files, eBooks, discount offers, and more

For support files and downloads related to your book, please visit www.PacktPub.com.

Did you know that Packt offers eBook versions of every book published, with PDF and ePub files available? You can upgrade to the eBook version at www.PacktPub.com and as a print book customer, you are entitled to a discount on the eBook copy. Get in touch with us at service@packtpub.com for more details.

At www.PacktPub.com, you can also read a collection of free technical articles, sign up for a range of free newsletters and receive exclusive discounts and offers on Packt books and eBooks.

https://www2.packtpub.com/books/subscription/packtlib

Do you need instant solutions to your IT questions? PacktLib is Packt's online digital book library. Here, you can search, access, and read Packt's entire library of books.

Why subscribe?

- Fully searchable across every book published by Packt
- Copy and paste, print, and bookmark content
- On demand and accessible via a web browser

Free access for Packt account holders

If you have an account with Packt at www.PacktPub.com, you can use this to access PacktLib today and view 9 entirely free books. Simply use your login credentials for immediate access.

Table of Contents

Preface

Welcome to the connected world. In the information age, everything around us is based on entities, relations, and above all, connectivity. Data is becoming exponentially more complex, which is affecting the performance of existing data stores. The most natural form in which data is visualized is in the form of graphs. In recent years, there has been an explosion of technologies to manage, process, and analyze graphs. While companies such as Facebook and LinkedIn have been the most well-known users of graph technologies for social web properties, a quiet revolution has been spreading across other industries. More than 30 of the Forbes Global 2000 companies, and many times as many start-ups have quietly been working to apply graphs to a wide array of business-critical use cases.

Neo4j, a graph database by Neo Technologies, is the leading player in the market for handling related data. It is not only efficient and easier to use, but it also includes all security and reliability features of tabulated databases.

We are entering an era of connected data where companies that can master the connections between their data—the lines and patterns linking the dots and not just the dots—will outperform the organizations that fail to recognize connectedness. It will be a long time before relational databases ebb into oblivion. However, their role is no longer universal. Graph databases are here to stay, and for now, Neo4j is setting the standard for the rest of the market.

This book presents an insight into how Neo4j can be applied to practical industry scenarios and also includes tweaks and optimizations for developers and administrators to make their systems more efficient and high performing.

What this book covers

Chapter 1, *Getting Started with Neo4j*, introduces Neo4j, its functionality, and norms in general, briefly outlining the fundamentals. The chapter also gives an overview of graphs, NOSQL databases and their features and Neo4j in particular, ACID compliance, basic CRUD operations, and setup. So, if you are new to Neo4j and need a boost, this is your chapter.

Chapter 2, *Querying and Indexing in Neo4j*, deals with querying Neo4j using Cypher, optimizations to data model and queries for better Cypher performance. The basics of Gremlin are also touched upon. Indexing in Neo4j and its types are introduced along with how to migrate from existing SQL stores and data import/export techniques.

Chapter 3, *Efficient Data Modeling with Graphs*, explores the data modeling concepts and techniques associated with graph data in Neo4j, in particular, property graph model, design constraints for Neo4j, the designing of schemas, and modeling across multiple domains.

Chapter 4, *Neo4j for High-volume Applications*, teaches you how to develop applications with Neo4j to handle high volumes of data. We will define how to develop an efficient architecture and transactions in a scalable way. We will also take a look at built-in graph algorithms for better traversals and also introduce Spring Data Neo4j.

Chapter 5, *Testing and Scaling Neo4j Applications*, teaches how to test Neo4j applications using the built-in tools and the GraphAware framework for unit and performance tests. We will also discuss how a Neo4j application can scale.

Chapter 6, *Neo4j Internals*, takes a look under the hood of Neo4j, skimming the concepts from the core classes in the source into the internal storage structure, caching, transactions, and related operations. Finally, the chapter deals with HA functions and master election.

Chapter 7, *Administering Neo4j*, throws light upon some useful tools and adapters that have been built to interface Neo4j with the most popular languages and frameworks. The chapter also deals with tips and configurations for administrators to optimize the performance of the Neo4j system. The essential security aspects are also dealt with in this chapter.

Chapter 8, *Use Case – Similarity-based Recommendation System*, is an example-oriented chapter. It provides a demonstration on how to go about building a similarity-based recommendation system with Neo4j and highlights the utility of graph visualization.

What you need for this book

This book is written for developers who work on machines based on Linux, Mac OS X, or Windows. All prerequisites are described in the first chapter to make sure your system is Neo4j-enabled and meets a few requirements. In general, all the examples should work on any platform.

This book assumes that you have a basic understanding of graph theory and are familiar with the fundamental concepts of Neo4j. It focuses primarily on using Neo4j for production environments and provides optimization techniques to gain better performance out of your Neo4j-based application. However, beginners can use this book as well, as we have tried to provide references to basic concepts in most chapters. You will need a server with Windows, Linux, or Mac and the Neo4j Community edition or HA installed. You will also need Python and py2neo configured.

Lastly, keep in mind that this book is not intended to replace online resources, but rather aims at complementing them. So, obviously you will need Internet access to complete your reading experience at some points, through provided links.

Who this book is for

This book was written for developers who wish to go further in mastering the Neo4j graph database. Some sections of the book, such as the section on administering and scaling, are targeted at database admins.

It complements the usual "Introducing Neo4j" reference books and online resources and goes deeper into the internal structure and large-scale deployments.

It also explains how to write and optimize your Cypher queries. The book concentrates on providing examples with Java and Cypher. So, if you are not using graph databases or using an adapter in a different language, you will probably learn a lot through this book as it will help you to understand the working of Neo4j.

This book presents an example-oriented approach to learning the technology, where the reader can learn through the code examples and make themselves ready for practical scenarios both in development and production. The book is basically the "how-to" for those wanting a quick and in-depth learning experience of the Neo4j graph database.

While these topics are quickly evolving, this book will not become obsolete that easily because it rather focuses on whys instead of hows. So, even if a given tool presented is not used anymore, you will understand why it was useful and you will be able to pick the right tool with a critical point of view.

Conventions

In this book, you will find a number of styles of text that distinguish between different kinds of information. Here are some examples of these styles, and an explanation of their meaning.

Code words in text are shown as follows: "This is equivalent to the `assertSubGraph()` method of the GraphUnit API."

A block of code is set as follows:

```
<dependency>
<groupId>org.Neo4j</groupId>
<artifactId>Neo4j-kernel</artifactId>
<version>2.1.4</version>
<scope>test</scope>
<type>test-jar</type>
</dependency>
```

Any command-line input or output is written as follows:

```
# sudo service neo4j-service status
```

New terms and **important words** are shown in bold. Words that you see on the screen, in menus or dialog boxes for example, appear in the text like this: "Click on **Finish** to complete the package addition process."

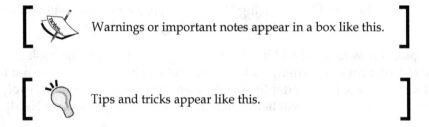

> Warnings or important notes appear in a box like this.

> Tips and tricks appear like this.

Reader feedback

Feedback from our readers is always welcome. Let us know what you think about this book—what you liked or disliked. Reader feedback is important for us as it helps us develop titles that you will really get the most out of.

To send us general feedback, simply e-mail feedback@packtpub.com, and mention the book's title in the subject of your message.

If there is a topic that you have expertise in and you are interested in either writing or contributing to a book, see our author guide at www.packtpub.com/authors.

Customer support

Now that you are the proud owner of a Packt book, we have a number of things to help you to get the most from your purchase.

Downloading the example code

You can download the example code files from your account at http://www.packtpub.com for all the Packt Publishing books you have purchased. If you purchased this book elsewhere, you can visit http://www.packtpub.com/support and register to have the files e-mailed directly to you.

Errata

Although we have taken every care to ensure the accuracy of our content, mistakes do happen. If you find a mistake in one of our books—maybe a mistake in the text or the code—we would be grateful if you could report this to us. By doing so, you can save other readers from frustration and help us improve subsequent versions of this book. If you find any errata, please report them by visiting http://www.packtpub.com/submit-errata, selecting your book, clicking on the **Errata Submission Form** link, and entering the details of your errata. Once your errata are verified, your submission will be accepted and the errata will be uploaded to our website or added to any list of existing errata under the Errata section of that title.

To view the previously submitted errata, go to https://www.packtpub.com/books/content/support and enter the name of the book in the search field. The required information will appear under the **Errata** section.

Piracy

Piracy of copyrighted material on the Internet is an ongoing problem across all media. At Packt, we take the protection of our copyright and licenses very seriously. If you come across any illegal copies of our works in any form on the Internet, please provide us with the location address or website name immediately so that we can pursue a remedy.

Please contact us at copyright@packtpub.com with a link to the suspected pirated material.

We appreciate your help in protecting our authors and our ability to bring you valuable content.

Questions

If you have a problem with any aspect of this book, you can contact us at questions@packtpub.com, and we will do our best to address the problem.

1

Getting Started with Neo4j

Graphs and graph operations have grown into prime areas of research in computer science. One reason for this is that graphs can be useful in representing several, otherwise abstract, problems in existence today. Representing the solution space of the problem in terms of graphs can trigger innovative approaches to solving such problems. It's simple. Everything around us, that is, everything we come across in our day-to-day life can be represented as graphs, and when your whiteboard sketches can be directly transformed into data structures, the possibilities are limitless. Before we dive into the technicalities and utilities of graph databases with the topics covered in this chapter, let's understand what graphs are and how representing data in the form of graph databases makes our lives easier. The following topics are dealt with in this chapter:

- Graphs and their use
- NoSQL databases and their types
- Neo4j properties, setup, and configurations
- Deployment on the Amazon and Azure cloud platforms

Graphs and their utilities

Graphs are a way of representing entities and the connections between them. Mathematically, graphs can be defined as collections of nodes and edges that denote entities and relationships. The nodes are data entities whose mutual relationships are denoted with the help of edges. Undirected graphs have two-way connections between edges whereas a directed graph has only a one-way edge between the nodes. We can also record the value of an edge and that is referred to as the weight of the graph.

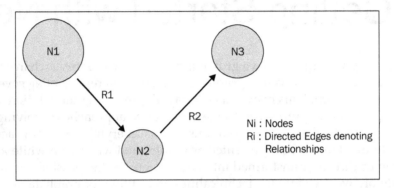

Modern datasets of science, government, or business are diverse and interrelated, and for years we have been developing data stores that have tabular schema. So, when it comes to highly connected data, tabular data stores offer retarded and highly complex operability. So, we started creating data stores that store data in the raw form in which we visualize them. This not only makes it easier to transform our ideas into schemas but the whiteboard friendliness of such data stores also makes it easy to learn, deploy, and maintain such data stores. Over the years, several databases were developed that stored their data structurally in the form of graphs. We will look into them in the next section.

Introducing NoSQL databases

Data has been growing in volume, changing more rapidly, and has become more structurally varied than what can be handled by typical relational databases. Query execution times increase drastically as the size of tables and number of joins grow. This is because the underlying data models build sets of probable answers to a query before filtering to arrive at a solution. **NoSQL** (often interpreted as **Not only SQL**) provides several alternatives to the relational model.

NoSQL represents the new class of data management technologies designed to meet the increasing volume, velocity, and variety of data that organizations are storing, processing, and analyzing. NoSQL comprises diverse different database technologies, and it has evolved as a response to an exponential increase in the volume of data stored about products, objects, and consumers, the access frequency of this data, along with increased processing and performance requirements. Relational databases, on the contrary, find it difficult to cope with the rapidly growing scale and agility challenges that are faced by modern applications, and they struggle to take advantage of the cheap, readily available storage and processing technologies in the market.

Often referred to as NoSQL, nonrelational databases feature elasticity and scalability. In addition, they can store big data and work with cloud computing systems. All of these factors make them extremely popular. NoSQL databases address the opportunities that the relational model does not, including the following:

- Large volumes of structure-independent data (including unstructured, semi-structured, and structured data)

- Agile development sprints, rapid iterations, and frequent repository pushes for the code

- Flexible, easy-to-use object-oriented programming

- Efficient architecture that is capable of scaling out, as compared to expensive and monolithic architectures due to the requirement of specialized hardware

Dynamic schemas

In the case of relational databases, you need to define the schema before you can add your data. In other words, you need to strictly follow a format for all data you are likely to store in the future. For example, you might store data about consumers such as phone numbers, first and last names, address including the city and state—a SQL database must be told what you are storing in advance, thereby giving you no flexibility.

Agile development approaches do not fit well with static schemas, since every completion of a new feature requires the schema of your database to change. So, after a few development iterations, if you decide to store consumers' preferred items along with their contact addresses and phone numbers, that column will need to be added to the already existing-database, and then migrate the complete database to an entirely new schema.

In the case of a large database, this is a time-consuming process that involves significant downtime, which might adversely affect the business as a whole. If the application data frequently changes due to rapid iterations, the downtime might be occurring quite often. Businesses sometimes wrongly choose relational databases in situations where the effective addressing of completely unstructured data is needed or the structure of data is unknown in advance. It is also worthy to note that while most NoSQL databases support schema or structure changes throughout their lifetime, some including graph databases adversely affect performance if schema changes are made after considerably large data has been added to the graph.

Automatic sharding

Because of their structure, relational databases are usually vertically scalable, that is, increasing the capacity of a single server to host more data in the database so that it is reliable and continuously available. There are limits to such scaling, both in terms of size and expense. An alternate approach is to scale horizontally by increasing the number of machines rather than the capacity of a single machine.

In most relational databases, **sharding** across multiple server instances is generally accomplished with **Storage Area Networks (SANs)** and other complicated arrangements that make multiple hardware act as a single machine. Developers have to manually deploy multiple relational databases across a cluster of machines. The application code distributes the data, queries, and aggregates the results of the queries from all instances of the database. Handling the failure of resources, data replication, and balancing require customized code in the case of manual sharding.

NoSQL databases usually support autosharding out of the box, which means that they natively allow the distribution of data stores across a number of servers, abstracting it from the application, which is unaware of the server pool composition. Data and query load are balanced automatically, and in the case of a node or server failure, it can quickly replace the failed node with no performance drop.

Cloud computing platforms such as Amazon Web Services provide virtually unlimited on-demand capacity. Hence, commodity servers can now provide the same storage and processing powers for a fraction of the price as a single high-end server.

Built-in caching

There are many products available that provide a cache tier to SQL database management systems. They can improve the performance of read operations substantially, but not that of write operations and moreover add complexity to the deployment of the system. If read operations, dominate the application, then distributed caching can be considered, but if write operations dominate the application or an even mix of read and write operations, then a scenario with distributed caching might not be the best choice for a good end user experience.

Most NoSQL database systems come with built-in caching capabilities that use the system memory to house the most frequently used data and doing away with maintaining a separate caching layer.

Replication

NoSQL databases support automatic replication, which means that you get high availability and failure recovery without the use of specialized applications to manage such operations. From the developer's perspective, the storage environment is essentially virtualized to provide a fault-tolerant experience.

Types of NoSQL databases

At one time, the answer to all your database needs was a relational database. With the rapidly spreading NoSQL database craze, it is vital to realize that different use cases and functionality call for a different database type. Based on the purpose of use, NoSQL databases have been classified in the following areas:

Key-value stores

Key-value database management systems are the most basic and fundamental implementation of NoSQL types. Such databases operate similar to a dictionary by mapping keys to values and do not reflect structure or relation. Key-value databases are usually used for the rapid storage of information after performing some operation, for example, a resource (memory)-intensive computation. These data stores offer extremely high performance and are efficient and easily scalable. Some examples of key-value data stores are **Redis** (in-memory data store with optional persistence.), **MemcacheDB** (distributed, in-memory key-value store), and **Riak** (highly distributed, replicated key-value store). Sounds interesting, huh? But how do you decide when to use such data stores?

Let's take a look at some key-value data store use cases:

- **Cache Data**: This is a type of rapid data storage for immediate or future use
- **Information Queuing**: Some key-value stores such as Redis support queues, sets, and lists for queries and transactions
- **Keeping live information**: Applications that require state management can use key-value stores for better performance
- **Distributing information or tasks**

Column family stores

Column family NoSQL database systems extend the features of key-value stores to provide enhanced functionality. Although they are known to have a complex nature, column family stores operate by the simple creation of collections of key-value pairs (single or many) that match a record. Contrary to relational databases, column family NoSQL stores are schema-less. Each record has one or more columns that contain the information with variation in each column of each record.

Column-based NoSQL databases are basically 2D arrays where each key contains a single key-value pair or multiple key-value pairs associated with it, thereby providing support for large and unstructured datasets to be stored for future use. Such databases are generally used when the simple method of storing key-value pairs is not sufficient and storing large quantities of records with a lot of information is mandatory. Database systems that implement a column-based, schema-less model are extremely scalable.

These data stores are powerful and can be reliably used to store essential data of large sizes. Although they are not flexible in what constitutes the data (such as related objects cannot be stored!), they are extremely functional and performance oriented. Some column-based data stores are **HBase** (an Apache Hadoop data store based on ideas from BigTable) and **Cassandra** (a data store based on DynamoDB and BigTable).

So, when do we want to use such data stores? Let's take a look at some use cases to understand the utility of column-based data stores:

- **Scaling**: Column family stores are highly scalable and can handle tons of information without affecting performance
- **Storing non-volatile, unstructured information**: If collections of attributes or values need to persist for extended time periods, column-based data stores are quite handy

Document databases

Document-based NoSQL databases are the latest craze that have managed to gain wide and serious acceptance in large enterprises recently. These DBMS operate in a similar manner to column-based data stores, incorporating the fact that they allow much deeper nesting of data to realize more complex data structures (for example, a hierarchal data format with a document, within another document, within a document). Unlike columnar databases that allow one or two levels of nesting, document databases have no restriction on the key-value nesting in documents. Any document with a complex and arbitrary structure can be stored using such data stores.

Although they have a powerful nature of storage, where you can use the individual keys for the purpose of querying records, document-based database systems have their own issues and drawbacks, for example, getting the whole record to retrieve a value of the record and similarly for updates that affect the performance in the long run.

Document-based databases are a viable choice for storing a lot of unrelated complex information with variable structure. Some document-based databases are **Couchbase** (a memcached compatible and JSON-based document database), **CouchDB**, and **MongoDB** (a popular, efficient, and highly functional database that is gaining popularity in big data scenarios).

Let's look at popular use cases associated with document databases to decide when to pick them as your tools:

- **Nested information handling**: These data stores are capable of handling data structures that are complex in nature and deeply nested
- **JavaScript compatible**: They interface easily with applications that use JavaScript-friendly JSON in data handling

Graph databases

A graph database exposes a graph model that has **create, read, update and delete (CRUD)** operation support. Graph databases are online (real time) in nature and are built generally for the purpose of being used in transactional (OLTP) systems. A graph database model represents data in a completely different fashion, unlike the other NoSQL models. They are represented in the form of tree-like structures or graphs that have nodes and edges that are connected to each other by relationships. This model makes certain operations easier to perform since they link related pieces of information.

Such databases are popular in applications that establish a connection between entities. For example, when using online social or professional networks, your connection to your friends and their friends' friends' relation to you are simpler to deal with when using graph databases. Some popular graph databases are **Neo4j** (a schema-less, extremely powerful graph database built in Java) and **OrientDB** (a speed-oriented hybrid NoSQL database of graph and document types written in Java; it is equipped with a variety of operational modes). Let's look at the use cases of graph databases:

- **Modeling and classification handling**: Graph databases are a perfect fit for situations involving related data. Data modeling and information classification based on related objects are efficient using this type of data store.

- **Complex relational information handling**: Graph databases ease the use of connection between entities and support extremely complex related objects to be used in computation without much hassle.

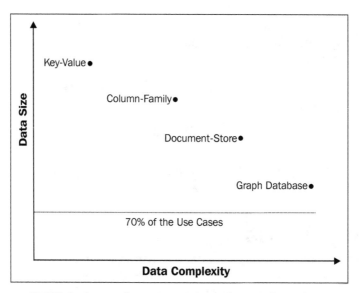

NoSQL database performance variation with size and complexity

The following criteria can help decide when the use of NoSQL databases is required depending on the situation in hand:

- **Data size matters**: When large datasets are something you are working on and have to deal with scaling issues, then databases of the NoSQL family should be an ideal choice.

- **Factor of speed**: Unlike relational databases, NoSQL data stores are considerably faster in terms of write operations. Reads, on the other hand, depend on the NoSQL database type being used and the type of data being stored and queried upon.

- **Schema-free design approach**: Relational databases require you to define a structure at the time of creation. NoSQL solutions are highly flexible and permit you to define schemas on the fly with little or no adverse effects on performance.

- **Scaling with automated and simple replications**: NoSQL databases are blending perfectly with distributed scenarios over time due to their built-in support. NoSQL solutions are easily scalable and work in clusters.

- **Variety of choices available**: Depending on your type of data and intensity of use, you can choose from a wide range of available database solutions to viably use your database management systems.

Graph compute engines

A graph compute engine is a technology that enables global graph computational algorithms to be run against large datasets. The design of graph compute engines basically supports things such as identifying clusters in data, or applying computations on related data to answer questions such as how many relationships, on average, does everyone on Facebook have? Or who has second-degree connections with you on LinkedIn?

Because of their emphasis on global queries, graph compute engines are generally optimized to scan and process large amounts of information in batches, and in this respect, they are similar to other batch analysis technologies, such as data mining and OLAP, that are familiar in the relational world. Whereas some graph compute engines include a graph storage layer, others (and arguably most of them) concern themselves strictly with processing data that is fed in from an external source and returning the results.

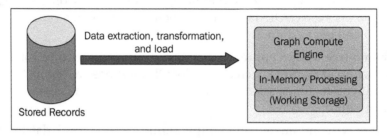

A high-level overview of a graph computation engine setup

The Neo4j graph database

Neo4j is one of the most popular graph databases today. It was developed by Neo Technology, Inc. operating from the San Francisco Bay Area in the U.S. It is written in Java and is available as open source software. Neo4j is an embedded, disk-based, fully transactional Java persistence engine that stores data structured in graphs rather than in tables. Most graph databases available have a storage format of two types:

- Most graph databases store data in the relational way internally, but they abstract it with an interface that presents operations, queries, and interaction with the data in a simpler and more graphical manner.

- Some graph databases such as Neo4j are native graph database systems. It means that they store the data in the form of nodes and relationships inherently. They are faster and optimized for more complex data.

In the following sections, we will see an overview of the Neo4j fundamentals, basic CRUD operations, along with the installation and configuration of Neo4j in different environments.

ACID compliance

Contrary to popular belief, **ACID** does not contradict or negate the concept of NoSQL. NoSQL fundamentally provides a direct alternative to the explicit schema in classical RDBMSes. It allows the developer to treat things asymmetrically, whereas traditional engines have enforced rigid sameness across the data model. The reason this is so interesting is because it provides a different way to deal with change, and for larger datasets, it provides interesting opportunities to deal with volumes and performance. In other words, the transition is about shifting the handling of complexity from the database administrators to the database itself.

Transaction management has been the talking point of NoSQL technologies since they started to gain popularity. The trade-off of transactional attributes for performance and scalability has been the common theme in nonrelational technologies that targeted big data. Some databases (for example, BigTable, Cassandra, and CouchDB) opted to trade-off consistency. This allowed clients to read stale data and in some cases, in a distributed system (eventual consistency), or in key-value stores that concentrated on read performance, where durability of the data was not of too much interest (for example, Memcached), or atomicity on a single-operation level, without the possibility to wrap multiple database operations within a single transaction, which is typical for document-oriented databases. Although devised a long time ago for relational databases, transaction attributes are still important in the most practical use cases. Neo4j has taken a different approach here. Neo4j's goal is to be a graph database, with the emphasis on database. This means that you'll get full ACID support from the Neo4j database:

- **Atomicity (A)**: This can wrap multiple database operations within a single transaction and make sure that they are all executed atomically; if one of the operations fails, a rollback is performed on the entire transaction.

- **Consistency (C)**: With this, when you write data to the Neo4j database, you can be sure that every client accessing the database afterwards will read the latest updated data.

- **Isolation (I)**: This will make sure that operations within a single transaction will be isolated one from another so that writes in one transaction won't affect reads in another transaction.

- **Durability (D)**: With this, you're certain that the data you write to Neo4j will be written to disk and available after a database restart or a server crash. If the system blows up (hardware or software), the database will pick itself back up.

The ACID transactional support provides seamless transition to Neo4j for anyone used to relational databases and offers safety and convenience in working with graph data.

Transactional support is one of the strong points of Neo4j, which differentiates it from the majority of NoSQL solutions and makes it a good option not only for NoSQL enthusiasts but also in enterprise environments. It is also one of the reasons for its popularity in big data scenarios.

Characteristics of Neo4j

Graph databases are built with the objective of optimizing transactional performance and are engineered to persist transactional integrity and operational availability. Two properties are useful to understand when investigating graph database technologies:

- **The storage within**: Some graph databases store data natively as graphs, which is optimized by design for storage, queries, and traversals. However, this is not practiced by all graph data stores. Some databases use serialization of the graph data into an equivalent general-purpose database including object-oriented and relational databases.

- **The processing engine**: Some graph databases definitions require that they possess the capability for index-free adjacency, which means that nodes that are connected must physically point to each other in the database. Here, let's take a broader view that any database which, from the user's perspective, behaves like a graph database (that is, exposes a graph data model through CRUD operations) qualifies as a graph database. However, there are significant performance advantages of leveraging index-free adjacency in graph data.

Graph databases, in particular native ones such as Neo4j, don't depend heavily on indexes because the graph itself provides a natural adjacency index. In a native graph database, the relationships attached to a node naturally provide a direct connection to other related nodes of interest. Graph queries largely involve using this locality to traverse through the graph, literally chasing pointers. These operations can be carried out with extreme efficiency, traversing millions of nodes per second, in contrast to joining data through a global index, which is many orders of magnitude slower. There are several different graph data models, including property graphs, hypergraphs, and triples. Let's take a brief look at them:

- **Property graphs**: A property graph has the following characteristics:
  - Being a graph, it has nodes and relationships
  - The nodes can possess properties (in the form of key-value pairs)
  - The relationships have a name and direction and must have a start and end node
  - The relationships are also allowed to contain properties

- **Hypergraphs**: A hypergraph is a generalized graph model in which a relationship (called hyperedge) can connect any number of nodes. Whereas the property graph model permits a relationship to have only one start node and one end node, the hypergraph model allows any number of nodes at either end of a relationship. Hypergraphs can be useful where the domain consists mainly of many-to-many relationships.

- **Triples**: Triple stores come from the Semantic Web movement, where researchers are interested in large-scale knowledge inference by adding semantic markup to the links that connect web resources. To date, very little of the web has been marked up in a useful fashion, so running queries across the semantic layer is uncommon. Instead, most efforts in the Semantic Web movement appear to be invested in harvesting useful data and relationship information from the web (or other more mundane data sources, such as applications) and depositing it in triple stores for querying.

Some essential characteristics of the Neo4j graph databases are as follows:

- They work well with web-based application scenarios including metadata annotations, wikis, social network analysis, data tagging, and other hierarchical datasets.

- It provides a graph-oriented model along with a visualization framework for the representation of data and query results.

- A decent documentation with an active and responsive e-mail list is a blessing for developers. It has a few releases and great utility indicating that it might last a while.

- Compatible bindings are written for most languages including Python, Java, Closure, and Ruby. Bindings for .NET are yet to be written. The REST interface is the recommended approach for access to the database.

- It natively includes a disk-based storage manager that has been completely optimized to store graphs to provide enhanced performance and scalability. It is also ready for SSDs.

- It is highly scalable. A single instance of Neo4j can handle graphs containing billions of nodes and relationships.

- It comes with a powerful traversal framework that is capable of handling speedy traversals in a graph space.

- It is completely transactional in nature. It is ACID compliant and supports features such as JTA or JTS, 2PC, XA, Transaction Recovery, Deadlock Detection, and so on.

- It is built to durably handle large graphs that don't fit in memory.
- Neo4j can traverse graph depths of more than 1,000 levels in a fraction of a second.

The basic CRUD operations

Neo4j stores data in entities called **nodes**. Nodes are connected to each other with the help of relationships. Both nodes and relationships can store properties or metadata in the form of key-value pairs. Thus, inherently a graph is stored in the database. In this section, we look at the basic CRUD operations to be used in working with Neo4j:

```
CREATE ( gates  { firstname: 'Bill', lastname: 'Gates'} )
```

```
CREATE ( page  { firstname: 'Larry', lastname: 'Page'}), (page) -
[r:WORKS_WITH] - > (gates)
```

```
RETURN gates, page, r
```

In this example, there are two queries; the first is about the creation of a node that has two properties. The second query performs the same operation as the first one, but also creates a relationship from `page` to `gates`.

```
START n=node(*) RETURN "The node count of the graph is "+count(*)+" !" as
ncount;
```

A variable named `ncount` is returned with the `The node count of the graph is 2!` value; it's basically the same as `select count(*)`.

```
START self=node(1) MATCH self<--friend
```

```
RETURN friend
```

Assuming that we are using this simple database as an example, these commands will return the `page` node keeping in mind the direction of the relationship:

```
START person=node(*)
```

```
MATCH person
```

```
WHERE person.firstname! ='Bill'
```

```
RETURN person
```

This query searches through all nodes and matches the ones with the `firstname` property that is equal to `Bill`. The `!` symbol makes sure that only nodes that possess the property are to be taken into consideration, to prevent errors.

```
START person=node(*)
MATCH person
WHERE person.firstname! ='Bill'
SET person.age = '60'
RETURN person
```

The node that has the `firstname` property as `Bill` is searched and adds another property called `age` that has the value `60`.

```
START person = node(*)
MATCH person
WHERE person.firstname! = "Larry"
DELETE person
```

In this query, we match all nodes that have `firstname` equal to `Larry` and perform a delete operation on them.

```
START node = node(*)
MATCH node-[r]-()
DELETE node, r
```

This query is used to fetch all nodes and relationships and performs a delete operation on them.

So, you now know how to perform basic CRUD operations on a Neo4j graph. We will encounter more of these queries in more complex forms in later chapters in the book.

The Neo4j setup and configurations

Neo4j is versatile in terms of usability. You can include and package Neo4j libraries in your application. This is referred to as the embedded mode of operation. For a server setup, you install Neo4j on the machine and configure it as an operating system service. The latest releases of Neo4j come with simple installer scripts for different operating systems. Let's take a look at how to configure Neo4j in the different modes of operation.

Modes of setup – the embedded mode

Neo4j in the embedded mode is used to include a graph database in your application. In this section, we will see how to configure Neo4j embedded into your application in Eclipse IDE. Ensure that you have the proper version of eclipse IDE from `https://www.eclipse.org/downloads/` and the Neo4j Enterprise edition TAR archive from the other downloads section at `http://www.neo4j.org/download`.

Within Eclipse, navigate to **File | New | Java Project**, give your project a preferred name, and then click on **Finish**.

Under the **Project Properties** page, select the option for **Java Build Path (1)** on the sidebar, proceed to the **Libraries** tab (**2**), and then click on the button for **Add External JARs** (**3**). You can now locate the external JAR files of the libraries you want to add from here.

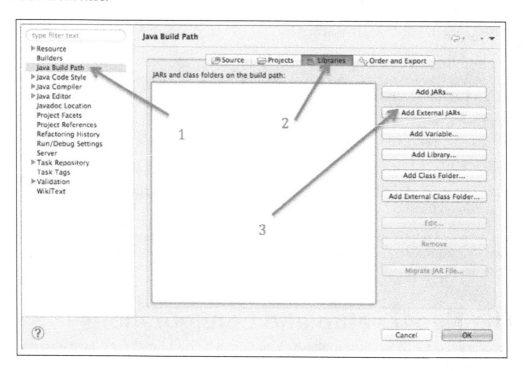

Navigate to the directory you extracted Neo4j under and look under the **libs** directory. Select all the ***.jar** files and click on **Add**. Click on **Finish** to complete the package addition process.

In the Eclipse navigation sidebar, right-click on the `src` folder of the newly created project and navigate to **New | Package**. In the dialog that appears, add a new package name. In the example, we have added `com.neo4j.chapter1`. Click on the **Finish** button.

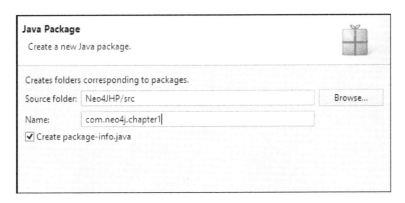

Right-click on the package created and create a new Java class by navigating to **New | Java Class** and name it accordingly (use `HelloNeo` to run the following example). Click on **Finish**. Add the following code into your project. This is a sample program to test whether our embedded setup is working fine:

```java
package com.neo4j.chapter1;

importorg.neo4j.graphdb.GraphDatabaseService;
import org.neo4j.graphdb.Node;
import org.neo4j.graphdb.Direction;
import org.neo4j.graphdb.Relationship;
import org.neo4j.graphdb.Transaction;
import org.neo4j.graphdb.RelationshipType;
import org.neo4j.graphdb.factory.GraphDatabaseFactory;

public class HelloNeo {
    //change the path according to your system and OS
    private static final String PATH_TO_DB = "path_to_your neo4j_
installation";

    String response;
    GraphDatabaseService graphDBase;
    Node node_one;
    Node node_two;
    Relationship relation;
```

```
    private static enum RelationTypes implements RelationshipType {
HATES }

  public static void main( final String[] args )
  {
      HelloNeo neoObject = new HelloNeo();
      neoObject.createGraphDb();
      neoObject.removeGraph();
      neoObject.shutDownDbServer();
  }

  void createGraphDb()
  {
      graphDBase = new GraphDatabaseFactory().newEmbeddedDatabase(
PATH_TO_DB );

      Transaction tx = graphDBase.beginTx();
      try
      {
          node_one = graphDBase.createNode();
          node_one.setProperty( "name", "Bill Gates, Microsoft" );
          node_two = graphDBase.createNode();
          node_two.setProperty( "name", "Larry Page, Google" );

          relation = node_one.createRelationshipTo( node_two,
RelationTypes.HATES );
          relation.setProperty( "relationship-type", "hates" );

          response = ( node_one.getProperty( "name" ).toString() )
                      + " " + ( relation.getProperty( "relationship-
type" ).toString() )
                      + " " + ( node_two.getProperty( "name"
).toString() );
          System.out.println(response);

          tx.success();
      }
      finally
      {
          tx.finish();
      }
  }

  void removeGraph()
  {
```

```
        Transaction tx = graphDBase.beginTx();
        try
        {
            node_one.getSingleRelationship( RelationTypes.HATES,
Direction.OUTGOING ).delete();
            System.out.println("Nodes are being removed . . .");
            node_one.delete();
            node_two.delete();
            tx.success();
        }
        finally
        {
            tx.finish();
        }
    }

    void shutDownDbServer()
    {
        graphDBase.shutdown();
        System.out.println("graphdb is shutting down.");
    }
}
```

On running the program, you will see the different stages of operation if your configuration is correct. In fact, there is an easier way to set up this configuration if you are familiar with Maven.

 Apache Maven is a software project management and comprehension tool. Based on the concept of **Project Object Model (POM)**, Maven can manage a project's build, reporting, and documentation from a central piece of information. You can learn more about Maven from the official website at http://maven.apache.org/.

Start a new Maven project on Eclipse and edit pom.xml to have the following lines for the dependencies:

```
<dependencies>
<dependency>
<groupId>junit</groupId>
<artifactId>junit</artifactId>
<version>3.8.1</version>
<scope>test</scope>
</dependency>
<dependency>
```

```
        <groupId>org.neo4j</groupId>
        <artifactId>neo4j</artifactId>
        <version>2.0.1</version>
    </dependency>
    </dependencies>
```

When you save the `pom.xml` file, the Neo4j dependencies are installed into the project. You can now run the preceding script and test the configuration.

Modes of setup – the server mode

To develop applications on single machines locally, the embedded database is efficient and serves the purpose. Most of the examples in this book can be tested with the embedded setup. However, for larger applications that deal with rapidly scaling data, the server mode of Neo4j provides the necessary functionality.

Setting up a Neo4j server is relatively easy. You can include Neo4j startup and shutdown as a normal operating system process. For most Linux distributions, the following procedure would suffice:

1. The latest release of Neo4j can be downloaded from `http://www.neo4j.org/download`. Select the compressed archive (`tar.gz`) distribution for your operating system.

2. The archive contents can be extracted using `tar -cf <filename>`.

   The master directory housing Neo4j can be referred to as `NEO4J_HOME`.

3. Move into the `$NEO4J_HOME` directory using `cd $NEO4J_HOME` and run the installer script using the following command:

   ```
   sudo ./bin/neo4j-installer install
   ```

4. If prompted, you will be required to enter your user password for super-user access privileges to restricted directories:

   ```
   sudo service neo4j-service status
   ```

   This indicates the state of the server, which in this case is `not running`.

5. The following command starts the Neo4j server:

   ```
   sudo service neo4j-service start
   ```

6. If you need to stop the server, you can run this from the terminal:

   ```
   sudo service neo4j-service stop
   ```

During installation, you will be asked to select the user under which Neo4j will. You can specify a username (the default is `neo4j`), and if that user does not exist on that system, a system account in that name will be created and the ownership of the `$NEO4J_HOME/data` directory will be assigned (chown) to that user. It is a good practice to create a dedicated user to run this service, and hence it is suggested that the downloaded archive is extracted under `/opt` or the package directory for optional packages on your system.

If you want the Neo4j server to no longer be a part of the system startup service, the following commands can be used to remove it:

```
cd $NEO4J_HOME
sudo ./bin/neo4j-installer remove
```

If the server is running, it is stopped and removed.

Neo4j high availability

In this section, we will learn how to set up Neo4j HA onto a production cluster. Let's assume that our cluster has three machines to be set up with Neo4j HA.

Download Neo4j Enterprise from `http://neo4j.org/download`, extract the archive into the machines on the production cluster, and perform the following configurations to the local property files of the HA servers:

Machine #1 – neo4j-01.local

File: `conf/neo4j.properties`:

```
# A unique Id for this machine, must be non-negative
ha.server_id = 1

# Specify other hosts that make up this database cluster.
ha.initial_hosts = neo4j-01.local:5001,neo4j-02.local:5001,neo4j-03.
local:5001

# You can also specify the hosts using their IP addresses
# ha.initial_hosts = 192.168.0.61:5001, 192.168.0.62:5001,
192.168.0.63:5001
```

File: conf/neo4j-server.properties:

```
# Mention the IP address to which this database server will listen
# to. 0.0.0.0 means it will listen to all incoming connections.
org.neo4j.server.webserver.address = 0.0.0.0

# Specify the mode of operation as HA if the mode is High
# Availability or set to SINGLE if using a cluster of 1 Node
# (This is default setting)
org.neo4j.server.database.mode=HA
```

Machine #2 – neo4j-02.local

File: conf/neo4j.properties:

```
# A unique Id for this machine, must be non-negative
ha.server_id = 2

# Specify other hosts that make up this database cluster.
ha.initial_hosts = neo4j-01.local:5001,neo4j-02.local:5001,neo4j-03.
local:5001

# You can also specify the hosts using their IP addresses
#ha.initial_hosts = 192.168.0.61:5001, 192.168.0.62:5001,
192.168.0.63:5001
```

File: conf/neo4j-server.properties:

```
# Mention the IP address to which this database server will listen
# to. 0.0.0.0 means it will listen to all incoming connections.
org.neo4j.server.webserver.address = 0.0.0.0

# Specify the mode of operation as HA if the mode is High
# Availability or set to SINGLE if using a cluster of 1 Node
# (This is default setting)
org.neo4j.server.database.mode=HA
```

Machine #3 – neo4j-03.local

File: conf/neo4j.properties:

```
# A unique Id for this machine, must be non-negative
ha.server_id = 3

# Specify other hosts that make up this database cluster.
```

```
ha.initial_hosts = neo4j-01.local:5001, neo4j-02.local:5001, neo4j-03.
local:5001

# You can also specify the hosts using their IP addresses
# ha.initial_hosts = 192.168.0.61:5001, 192.168.0.62:5001,
192.168.0.63:5001
```

File: conf/neo4j-server.properties:

```
# Mention the IP address to which this database server will listen
# to. 0.0.0.0 means it will listen to all incoming connections.
org.neo4j.server.webserver.address = 0.0.0.0

# Specify the mode of operation as HA if the mode is High
# Availability or set to SINGLE if using a cluster of 1 Node
# (This is default setting)
org.neo4j.server.database.mode = HA
```

Use the following commands on the neo4j script on each server to start up the servers. The order in which the servers are started is not important:

```
neo4j-01$ ./bin/neo4j start   (# to start first server)
neo4j-02$ ./bin/neo4j start   (# to start second server)
neo4j-03$ ./bin/neo4j start   (# to start third server)
```

If the database mode has been set to HA, the startup script does not wait for the server to become available, but returns immediately. The reason being that each machine does not accept requests till the setup of a cluster has been completed. For example, in the preceding configuration, this happens when the second machine starts up. In order to monitor the state of the startup process, you can trace messages in the console.log file created during the setup. You can find the location of the log file printed before the startup script terminates.

Configure Neo4j for Amazon clusters

The most popular thing among the cloud deployment platforms has been **Amazon Web Services (AWS)**, particularly on their EC2 cluster-computing systems. These services are not only easy to set up but offer a wide range of services and support that make the life of admins a lot easier in the long run.

Neo4j, like a lot of other databases, is quite easy to configure and set up on an AWS server. In this section, we outline the deployment process for a Neo4j instance on Amazon **EC2** (short for **Elastic Compute Cloud**). This process requires you to have a valid AWS account and be familiar with launching instances. If you feel you need to level up your experience with AWS, I would recommend that you follow the official guide of Amazon so that you are able to connect with your instance with SSH; the official guide is available at `http://docs.aws.amazon.com/AWSEC2/latest/UserGuide/EC2_GetStarted.html`.

You will also need a copy of the latest stable version of Neo4j for Unix Systems. The community edition will suffice for developmental purposes. The latest downloads can be found at `http://www.neo4j.org/download`. You can then perform the following steps:

1. You need to open the AWS management console and select **Ubuntu Server 12.04.1 LTS 64-bit** or start a basic 32-bit Linux instance. You could start an Ubuntu AMI but it does not include a Java installation, which is a key dependency of Neo4j, so you've got to install it manually.

2. In the **Instance Details** section, select **m1.large** as the type and make sure that **Availability Zone** is set to any of the **us-east** regions. A new security group needs to be created or you can use the default one and configure a new security rule for the port to be used by the Neo4j server.

3. When the instance is launched, a TCP rule is created on the 7474 port used by Neo4j with `0.0.0.0/0` as the source address. What we did was open the 7474 port for all external access (with `0.0.0.0` being the universal identifier). If you intend to use the Neo4j REST API by remote calls from another server, then for security reasons you can change the source field to that of the external server. The 22 port also needs to be open for SSH.

Now, it's time to install Neo4J into the system; let's do this by performing the following steps:

1. Open a terminal on your local system where we downloaded Neo4j. We now copy or transfer the archive to the AWS server using the `scp` command:

    ```
    scp -i filename.pem neo4j-community-2.1.2-unix.tar.gz ec2-user@
    PUBLIC_DNS_OF_INSTANCE:/home/ec2-user
    ```

2. You will need to provide the absolute path to your `pem` key file, which is typically found in `~/.ssh`, the filename of the Neo4j server, and the public DNS of your EC2 instance (`ec2-user` by default). Next, we establish a connection with our EC2 instance using SSH:

    ```
    ssh -i filename.pem ec2-user@PUBLIC_DNS_OF_INSTANCE
    ```

3. Extract the archive contents for the Neo4j server:

```
tar xvfz neo4j-community-2.1.2-unix.tar.gz
```

4. You need to move the content into `/usr/local` and change the folder name to `neo4j`:

```
sudo mv neo4j-community-2.1.2-unix.tar.gz /usr/local/neo4j
```

5. You now need to enable external access to the Neo4j server by editing the Neo4j configurations file. You need to open `neo4j-server.properties` under the `conf` directory of the master folder and append the following line:

```
org.neo4j.server.webserver.address = 0.0.0.0
```

This creates an open connection for anyone to access the Neo4j server. For restricted access, you can specify the IP of the machine, which will act as the source.

6. Finally, the server is started from the installation directory using the following command:

```
sudo ./bin/neo4j start
```

A startup script can be created to automate the server initiation. To check whether the deployment succeeded, you need to pop up a browser on your local machine and key in `http://PUBLIC_DNS_OF_INSTANCE:7474`.

This should direct you to the Monitoring and Management console of Neo4j on your AWS server. Voilà! We're done.

Cloud deployment with Azure

In this section, you will learn how to deploy Neo4j to a Linux VM hosted on Azure. Azure has wizards to guide you, but we will be using **Command-line Interface (CLI)** tools for our setup. If CLI tools are not installed on the system, you can install them using the Node package manager with the following command:

```
npm install azure-cli
```

When the tools are installed, we open a terminal, type `azure`, and we are greeted with cool ASCII art and some common commands. Now, to create our new Linux VM on Azure, we need the following information:

- The DNS name of our VM, which will later be used to access your app as `DNS_name.cloudapp.net`. We will be using `myDNS`.

- The name of an existing Ubuntu distribution image that can be selected from existing ones (type `azure vm image list` to view all images) or a custom image can be uploaded. Here, we use `z12k89b3b3w66g78t94rvd5b73dsrd23__Ubuntu-12_04_1-LTS-amd64-server-20140618-en-us-50GB`.

You can now create the Linux VM with the following command in the terminal:

```
azure vm create myDNS  z12k89b3b3w66g78t94rvd5b73dsrd23__Ubuntu-12_04_1-
LTS-amd64-server-20140618-en-us-50GB username -e -l "West US"
```

In this command, `username` is the default user account that will be created whose username is specified later. The `-e` flag enables SSH on the default port 22. The `-l` flag permits specifying the region where the VM will be deployed. Now we have the VM created and we can easily access it with SSH.

```
ssh username@myDNS.cloudapp.net
```

Since we are using an Ubuntu instance, we will install Neo4j using the Debian repository by performing the following steps:

1. Add the repository to your system configuration:

   ```
   echo 'deb http://debian.neo4j.org/repo stable/' > /etc/apt/
   sources.list.d/neo4j.list
   ```

2. The dependency list needs to be refreshed with the following command:

   ```
   sudo apt-get update
   ```

3. Neo4j is installed using the following command:

   ```
   Sudo apt-get install neo4j
   ```

If we need to access Neo4j from external applications or servers, we need to configure the Neo4j properties accordingly by performing the following steps:

1. Open the `/etc/neo4j/neo4j-server.properties` file. Add the following line to the file:

   ```
   org.neo4j.server.webserver.address = 0.0.0.0
   ```

2. Also, confirm that the SSL port is enabled:

   ```
   org.neo4j.server.webserver.https.enabled = true
   ```

If the server was already started, we need to restart it with the following command:

```
sudo /etc/init.d/neo4j-service restart
```

We will now navigate to the Azure portal and the port that Neo4j runs on (7474 by default) has to be opened if the server is intended to be used as a database server. In this case, we map the 7474 port with the 80 port so that the port need not be specified with the requests. We will be using the `add new endpoint` function of Azure for this, as shown below:

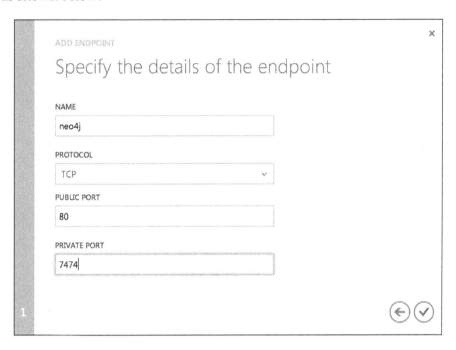

In order to test whether our installed application has successfully deployed, we can test it with the following call:

```
curl http://myDNS.cloudapp.net
```

If it works, we have successfully set up Neo4j on Azure. However, the fun does not end there. If your Azure subscription gives you access to apps for the Azure store, then you will find that Neo4j has been included as an app there. So, the first thing you need to do is install Apps for Azure.

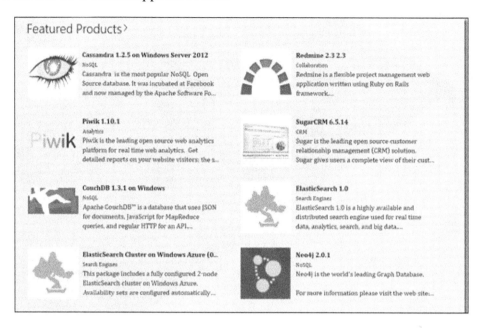

Search and select the latest version of Neo4j that is available in the store and then click on **Deploy To Cloud** in the screen that appears. We then need to select the data center and provide our Windows Azure Subscription details in the form of our `publishsettings` file.

We then select the size of our VM and specify a password for the administrator that will be mailed after the completion of the deployment.

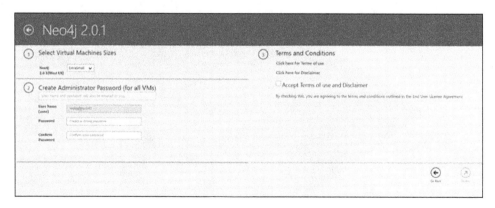

Next, once the deployment completes, you can RDP into the VM using the admin credentials from `http://manage.windowsazure.com`. Similar to the previous process, if we want our server to be accessible from external hosts, we will need to add the following line to the `neo4j-server.properties` file:

```
org.neo4j.server.webserver.address = 0.0.0.0
```

Summary

In this chapter, you learned about what NoSQL databases are and how important a role graph databases play when datasets are large, complex, and inter-related. You also learned about the different modes of operation of Neo4j, namely, embedded, server, and high availability, and how to configure each of them. Also, Neo4j is easy to set up in cloud deployment environments such as Amazon Clusters and Windows Azure, which offer native built-in support for Neo4j as a scalable database management system.

In the next chapter, we will be dealing with how to efficiently query Neo4j and also study the indexing support that can be used to optimize traversals.

2
Querying and Indexing in Neo4j

From what we learned in the previous chapter, we can say that while a relational database can be used to obtain the average age of all the people in a room, a graph database can indicate who is most likely to buy a drink. So, the utility of graph databases in the information age is vital.

In this chapter, we are going to take a look at the querying and indexing features of Neo4j and focus on the following areas:

- The Neo4j web interface
- Cypher queries and their optimization
- Introduction to Gremlin
- Indexing in Neo4j
- Migration techniques for SQL users

The Neo4j interface

Neo4j comes with a browser-based web interface with the ability to manage your database, run queries in Cypher or REST, as well as visualization support for graphs. You can view the status of your database with a node and the relationship count and disk usage stats under dashboard. The data browser helps you to run queries and visualize the results in the form of a graph. You can use the console option to run queries on the database. Cypher and REST are supported in the console of the web interface. Gremlin support was deprecated in the recent version but you can always use it as a powerful external tool. Overall, the web interface provides developers with an easy-to-use system with a frontend for monitoring and querying.

Running Cypher queries

The default page when you open Neo4j is `http://localhost:7474/browser/`, and it is an interactive shell in the browser to execute your queries in a single or multiline format. You can also view the results locally in the timeline format along with tables or visualizations depending upon the query. Queries can be saved using the star button in the pane and the current content in the editor will be saved. Drag and drop of scripts for stored queries or data import is also possible in this interface.

For administrative purposes, you can redirect to the webadmin interface at `http://localhost:7474/webadmin/`, which houses several features and functions that can be used to manage and monitor your database system.

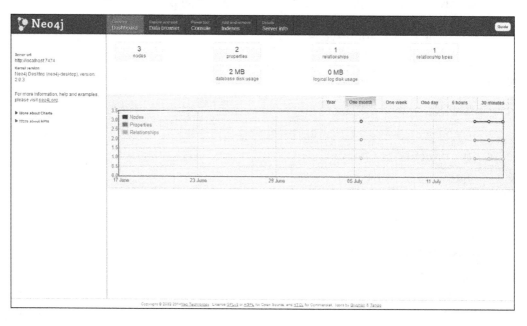

The Neo4j webadmin interface

Visualization of results

The most fascinating way of interacting with graphs is visualization. When you run Cypher queries, the result set is generally made up of nodes and relationships that are viewed in the data browser. Clicking on a node or a relationship in the visualizations will show a popup that contains the properties of that entity.

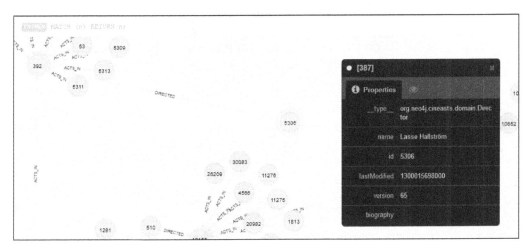

Visualization of results

You can also customize the content and colors, based on the label or type of relationship. A *label* is a named graph construct that is used to group nodes or relationships into sets; all nodes labeled with the same *label* belong to the same set. A *type* refers to different types of relationships that are present in the graph. (This is different from __type__, which is a property in Spring Data Neo4j used to map objects to nodes/relationships.) The elegance and design of Neo4j comes from the fact that every interaction that we have with it is a demonstration. It not only has a fluid and interactive UI but also a high-end administrative functionality.

Introduction to Cypher

Cypher is a graph query language that is declarative in nature. It supports expressive, efficient execution of queries and the updating of data on graph data stores. Cypher has a simple query construct but its power lies in the fact that we can express very complicated queries in a simple visual manner. This helps a developer to focus on the problem domain rather than worry about access issues of the database.

Cypher as a query language is humane by design. It is developer friendly as well as easily usable by an operations professional. Cypher's goal is making simple things easy and complex things possible; it bases its constructs on basic English prose, which makes queries increasingly self-explanatory. Since it is declarative in nature, Cypher emphasizes on expressing clearly what data has to be fetched from a graph, rather than how it is to be fetched, unlike most scripting and imperative languages such as Gremlin, or general-purpose programming languages such as Ruby or Java. In this approach, the optimization of queries becomes an implementation issue instead of going for the on-the-fly "updation" of traversals when the underlying structure or indexing of a database changes.

The Cypher syntax has been inspired by some well-established approaches for efficient querying. Some keywords in Cypher such as ORDER BY and WHERE are similar in functionality to those used in SQL. SPARQL-like (a primitive graph query language by Google) approaches for the matching of patterns have been adopted in Cypher; languages such as Python and Haskell have also inspired certain semantics.

Cypher graph operations

Cypher is a whiteboard-friendly language. Like the data on which it is used, queries in Cypher follow a diagrammatic approach in their syntax. This helps to target the use of graph databases to a greater variety of audience including database admins, developers, corporate professionals, and even the common folk. Let's take a look at some Cypher queries before diving into the best practices and optimizations for Cypher.

The following pattern shown depicts three entities interrelated through a relationship denoting the NEEDS dependency. It is represented in the form of an ASCII art:

```
(A)-[:NEEDS]->(B)-[:NEEDS]->(C),  (A)-[:NEEDS]->(C)
```

The previous statement is in the form of a path that links entity A to B, then B to C, and finally A to C. The directed relation is denoted with the -> operator. As it is evident, patterns denoted in Cypher are a realization of how graphs are represented on a whiteboard. It is worth noting that although a graph can be constructed with edges in both directions, the query-processing languages operate in one direction, for example, from left to right as in the preceding case. This is handled using a list of patterns that are separated with commas. Cypher queries fundamentally make use of patterns of the ASCII art. What a cypher query does is hold on to some initiating part of the graph with a section of its pattern and then use the remaining parts of the pattern to search for local matching entities in the graph.

Cypher clauses

Being a language for querying data, Cypher consists of several clauses to perform different tasks. A simple basic operation with cypher makes use of the START clause to anchor to the source, which is succeeded by a MATCH clause that is used to conditionally traverse through desired nodes in the graph and finally a RETURN clause that outputs the matching values or some computable action result. In the following query, we find a connecting flight path for the city of Alabama using Cypher:

```
START city1=node:location(name='Alabama')
MATCH (city1)-[:CONNECTS]->(city2)-[:CONNECTS]->(city3), (city1)-
[:CONNECTS]->(city3)
RETURN city2, city3
```

The preceding snippet contains the following three clauses:

- **The START clause**: This clause is used to indicate single or multiple starting points for the graph in consideration. The starting points in consideration can be nodes or relationships. We can look the start nodes up with the help of an index or occasionally accessed through the IDs of some node or relationship. In the previous query, we obtain the initial node with the help of an index called location that is asked to locate a place stored with the name property set to 'Alabama'. This statement returns a reference that we bind to an identifier called city1 in the previous example.

- **The MATCH clause**: These statements indicate that Cypher matches the pattern given with the initial identifier through the rest of the graph for find a match for the pattern. This way, we retrieve the data that we desire. Nodes are drawn with a set of parentheses and the relationships are indicated with the help of the --> and <-- symbols that also include the direction in which the relationship exists. Within the dashes in the previous symbols for relationships, we can insert the names of the relationships within a set of [...] and the name of the connecting relationship can be indicated after a colon.

  Since the pattern in the MATCH clause can occur in many ways, and if the size of the dataset is increased manifold, we will get a very large set of matched results. To avoid this, we use anchoring for a part of the pattern with the help of the START clause.

  The Cypher engine can then match the rest of the querying pattern in the graph surrounding the initiating points or nodes.

- **The RETURN clause**: The RETURN clause is used to specify the resulting nodes and connecting relationships that matched the pattern along with their properties in the form of identifiers, which in the previous example matched instances of city2 and city3. This follows a lazy binding approach for all the nodes that matched to some identifier that is specified in the query as the traversals take place in the graph.

More useful clauses

Some other essential clauses that Cypher supports for the construction of complex queries in the graph are listed as follows:

- CREATE: You can use this clause to define a new node or a new relationship. If you want only unique occurrences of nodes/relationships in the graphs, then you can use the CREATE UNIQUE clause to avoid the creation of duplicate entities.

- MERGE: This clause is equivalent to MATCH or CREATE. It can also be used with the help of indexes and unique constraints to find an existing entity or otherwise create a new one.

- WHERE: This clause provides a specification of conditions that can be used to filter nodes and relationships based on their stored properties.

- SET: This clause is used to assign values to properties of nodes or relationships.

- WITH: This clause is used to pipeline the output of one query in the form of input into the next query, thereby making the chaining of queries possible.

- UNION: This clause acts as a conjunction operation for queries in Cypher. You can combine the action of multiple queries on the data to produce a final result with the help of this clause.

- DELETE: It is used for the removal of any type of entities in the graph, be it nodes or relationships or their individual properties.

- FOREACH: This is an action clause that can be used to sequentially update the elements in a set of entities.

Some of these query clauses are radically similar to those in SQL. Cypher is intended to be simple enough so that it can be easily and quickly grasped by developers. Its clauses indicate that the operations are applied on graphs instead of relational data stores. We'll deal with some more clause-based examples in due course in the chapter.

Advanced Cypher tricks

Cypher is a highly efficient language that not only makes querying simpler but also strives to optimize the result-generation process to the maximum. A lot more optimization in performance can be achieved with the help of knowledge related to the data domain of the application being used to restructure queries.

Query optimizations

There are certain techniques you can adopt in order to get the maximum performance out of your Cypher queries. Some of them are:

- **Avoid global data scans**: The manual mode of optimizing the performance of queries depends on the developer's effort to reduce the traversal domain and to make sure that only the essential data is obtained in results. A global scan searches the entire graph, which is fine for smaller graphs but not for large datasets. For example:

```
START n =node(*)
MATCH (n)-[:KNOWS]-(m)
WHERE n.identity = "Batman"
RETURN m
```

Since Cypher is a greedy pattern-matching language, it avoids discrimination unless explicitly told to. Filtering data with a start point should be undertaken at the initial stages of execution to speed up the result-generation process.

 In Neo4j versions greater than 2.0, the START statement in the preceding query is not required, and unless otherwise specified, the entire graph is searched.

The use of labels in the graphs and in queries can help to optimize the search process for the pattern. For example:

```
START n =node(*)
MATCH (n:superheroes)-[:KNOWS]-(m)
WHERE n.identity = "Batman"
RETURN m
```

Using the superheroes label in the preceding query helps to shrink the domain, thereby making the operation faster. This is referred to as a label-based scan.

- **Indexing and constraints for faster search**: Searches in the graph space can be optimized and made faster if the data is indexed, or we apply some sort of constraint on it. In this way, the traversal avoids redundant matches and goes straight to the desired index location. To apply an index on a label, you can use the following:

```
CREATE INDEX ON: superheroes(identity)
```

Otherwise, to create a constraint on the particular property such as making the value of the property unique so that it can be directly referenced, we can use the following:

```
CREATE CONSTRAINT ON n:superheroes
ASSERT n.identity IS UNIQUE
```

We will learn more about indexing, its types, and its utilities in making Neo4j more efficient for large dataset-based operations in the next sections.

- **Avoid Cartesian Products Generation**: When creating queries, we should include entities that are connected in some way. The use of unspecific or nonrelated entities can end up generating a lot of unused or unintended results. For example:

```
MATCH  (m:Game), (p:Player)
```

This will end up mapping all possible games with all possible players and that can lead to undesired results. Let's use an example to see how to avoid Cartesian products in queries:

```
MATCH ( a:Actor), (m:Movie), (s:Series)
RETURN COUNT(DISTINCT a), COUNT(DISTINCT m), COUNT(DISTINCTs)
```

This statement will find all possible triplets of the `Actor`, `Movie`, and `Series` labels and then filter the results. An optimized form of querying will include successive counting to get a final result as follows:

```
MATCH (a:Actor)
WITH COUNT(a) as actors
MATCH (m:Movie)
WITH COUNT(m) as movies, actors
MATCH (s:Series)
RETURN COUNT(s) as series, movies, actors
```

This increases the 10x improvement in the execution time of this query on the same dataset.

- **Use more patterns in MATCH rather than WHERE**: It is advisable to keep most of the patterns used in the MATCH clause. The WHERE clause is not exactly meant for pattern matching; rather it is used to filter the results when used with START and WITH. However, when used with MATCH, it implements constraints to the patterns described. Thus, the pattern matching is faster when you use the pattern with the MATCH section. After finding starting points — either by using scans, indexes, or already-bound points — the execution engine will use pattern matching to find matching subgraphs. As Cypher is declarative, it can change the order of these operations. Predicates in WHERE clauses can be evaluated before, during, or after pattern matching.

- **Split MATCH patterns further**: Rather than having multiple match patterns in the same MATCH statement in a comma-separated fashion, you can split the patterns in several distinct MATCH statements. This process considerably decreases the query time since it can now search on smaller or reduced datasets at each successive match stage.

  When splitting the MATCH statements, you must keep in mind that the best practices include keeping the pattern with labels of the smallest cardinality at the head of the statement. You must also try to keep those patterns generating smaller intermediate result sets at the beginning of the match statements block.

- **Profiling of queries**: You can monitor your queries' processing details in the profile of the response that you can achieve with the PROFILE keyword, or setting profile parameter to True while making the request. Some useful information can be in the form of _db_hits that show you how many times an entity (node, relationship, or property) has been encountered.

  Returning data in a Cypher response has substantial overhead. So, you should strive to restrict returning complete nodes or relationships wherever possible and instead, simply return the desired properties or values computed from the properties.

- **Parameters in queries**: The execution engine of Cypher tries to optimize and transform queries into relevant execution plans. In order to optimize the amount of resources dedicated to this task, the use of parameters as compared to literals is preferred. With this technique, Cypher can re-utilize the existing queries rather than parsing or compiling the literal-hbased queries to build fresh execution plans:

```
MATCH (p:Player) -[:PLAYED]-(game)
WHERE p.id = {pid}
RETURN game
```

When Cypher is building execution plans, it looks at the schema to see whether it can find useful indexes. These index decisions are only valid until the schema changes, so adding or removing indexes leads to the execution plan cache being flushed.

Add the direction arrowhead in cases where the graph is to be queries in a directed manner. This will reduce a lot of redundant operations.

Graph model optimizations

Sometimes, the query optimizations can be a great way to improve the performance of the application using Neo4j, but you can incorporate some fundamental practices while you define your database so that it can make things easier and faster for usage:

- **Explicit definition:** If the graph model we are working upon contains implicit relationships between components. A higher efficiency in queries can be achieved when we define these relations in an explicit manner. This leads to faster comparisons but it comes with a drawback that now the graph would require more storage space for an additional entity for all occurrences of data. Let's see this in action with the help of an example.

  In the following diagram, we see that when two players have played in the same game, they are most likely to know each other. So, instead of going through the game entity for every pair of connected players, we can define the **KNOWS** relationship explicitly between the players.

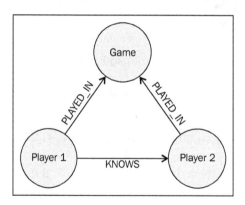

- **Property refactoring**: This refers to the situation where complex time-consuming operations in the WHERE or MATCH clause can be included directly as properties in the nodes of the graph. This not only saves computation time resulting in much faster queries but it also leads to more organized data storage practices in the graph database for utility. For example:

```
MATCH (m:Movie)
WHERE m.releaseDate >1343779201 AND m.releaseDate< 1369094401
RETURN m
```

This query is to compare whether a movie has been released in a particular year; it can be optimized if the release year of the movie is inherently stored in the properties of the movie nodes in the graph as the year range 2012-2013. So, for the new format of the data, the query will now change to this:

```
MATCH (m:Movie)-[:CONTAINS]->(d)
WHERE s.name = "2012-2013"
RETURN g
```

This gives a marked improvement in the performance of the query in terms of its execution time.

Gremlin – an overview

Gremlin is basically a wrapper to Groovy. It provides some nice constructs that make the traversal of graphs efficient. It is an expressive language written by Marko Rodriguez and uses connected operations for the traversal of a graph. Gremlin can be considered *Turing complete* and has simple and easy-to-understand syntax.

 Groovy is a powerful, optionally typed, and dynamic language, with static typing and static compilation capabilities for the Java platform aimed at multiplying developers' productivity thanks to a concise, familiar, and easy-to-learn syntax. It integrates smoothly with any Java program and immediately delivers to your application powerful features, including scripting capabilities, domain-specific language authoring, runtime and compile-time meta-programming, and functional programming. Check it out at http://groovy-lang.org/.

Gremlin integrates well with Neo4j since it was mainly designed for use with property graphs. The earlier versions sported the Gremlin console on the web interface shell, but the latest version does away with it. Gremlin is generally used with an REPL or a command line to make traversals on a graph interactively.

Let's browse through some useful queries in Gremlin for graph traversals.

You can set up the Gremlin REPL to test out the queries. Download the latest build from `https://github.com/tinkerpop/gremlin/wiki/Downloads` and follow the setup instructions given on the official website. Now, in order to configure your Gremlin with your Neo4j installation, you need to first create a `neo4j.groovy` file with the path to your `neo4j/data/graph.db` directory and add the following lines:

```
// neo4j.groovy
import org.neo4j.kernel.EmbeddedReadOnlyGraphDatabase
db = new EmbeddedReadOnlyGraphDatabase('/path/to/neo4j/data/graph.db')
g = new Neo4jGraph(db)
```

When you start a new Gremlin REPL, you will need to load this file in order to use Gremlin commands with your Neo4j database:

```
$ cd /path/to/gremlin
$ ./gremlin.sh


         \,,,/
         (o o)
-----o0Oo-(_)-oO0o-----
gremlin> load neo4j.groovy
gremlin>
```

You can now try out some of the Gremlin clauses mentioned in the following points:

- You can connect to an existing instance of a graph database such as Neo4j with the help of the following command at the Gremlin prompt:

  ```
  gremlin>  g = new Neo4jGraph ("/path/to/database")
  ```

- If you want to view all the nodes or vertices and edges in the graph, you can use the following commands:

  ```
  gremlin>  g.V
  gremlin>  g.E
  ```

- To get a particular vertex that has been indexed, type the following command. It returns the vertex that has a property name "Bill Gates" as the name. Since the command returns an iterator, the `>>` symbol is used to pop the next item in the iterator and assign it to the variable in consideration:

  ```
  gremlin> v =  g.idx(T.v)[[name: "Bill Gates"]] >> 1
  ==>v[165]
  ```

- To look at the properties on the particular vertex, you need the following command:

```
gremlin> v.map
==> name = Bill Gates
==> age = 60
==> designation = CEO
==> company = Microsoft
```

  To view the outgoing edges from that node, we use the following command. The result of that will print out all the outbound edges from that graph in the format that consists of the node indices:

```
e[212][165-knows->180]
==> v.outE
```

- You can also write very simple queries to retrieve the node at the other end of a relationship based on its label in the following manner:

```
gremlin> v.outE[[label:'knows']].inV.name
==> Steve Jobs
```

- Gremlin also allows you to trace the path it takes to achieve a particular result with the help of an in-built property. All you need to do is append a .path to the end of the query whose path you want to view:

```
gremlin> v.outE[[label:'knows']].inV.name.path
==> [v[165], e[212][ 165-knows->180], v[180], Steve Jobs]
```

- If we need to find the names of all the vertices in the graph that are known by the vertex with the ID 165 and that have exceeded 30 years. Note that conditions in the Gremlin statements are expressed in a pair of {} similar to that in Groovy:

```
gremlin>  v.outE{it.label=='knows'}.inV{it.age > 30}.name
```

- Finally, let's see how we can use collaborative filters on the vertex with the ID 165 to make calculations:

```
gremlin> m = [:]
gremlin> v.outE.inV.name.groupCount(m).back(2).loop(3){it.loops<4}
gremlin> m.sort{a,b -> a.value <=> b.value}
```

The preceding statements first create a map in Groovy called m. Next, we find all the outgoing edges from v, the incoming vertices at the end of those edges, and then the name property. Since we cannot get the outgoing edges of the name, we go back two steps to the actual vertex and then loop back three times in the statement to go to the required entity. This maps the count retrieved from the looping to the ID of the vertex and then stores them in the m map. The final statement sorts the results in the map based on the count value. So, Gremlin is quite interesting for quick tinkering with graph data and constructing small complex queries for analysis. However, since it is a Groovy wrapper for the Pipes framework, it lacks scope for optimizations or abstractions.

Indexing in Neo4j

In earlier builds, Neo4j had no support for indexing and was a simple property graph. However, as the datasets scaled in size, it was inconvenient and error-prone to traverse the entire graph for even the smallest of queries, so the need to effectively define the starting point of the graph had to be found. Hence, the need for indexing arose followed by the introduction of manual and then automatic indexing. Current versions of Neo4j have extensive support for indexing as part of their fundamental graph schema.

Manual and automatic indexing

Manual indexing was introduced in the early versions of Neo4j and was achieved with the help of the Java API. Automatic indexing was introduced from Neo4j 1.4. It's a manual index under the hood that contains a fixed name (node_auto_index, relationship_auto_index) combined with TransactionEventHandler that mirrors changes on index property name configurations. Automatic indexing is typically set up in neo4j.properties. This technique removes lot of burden from the manual mirroring of changes to the index properties, and it permits Cypher statements to alter the index implicitly. Every index is bound to a unique name specified by the user and can be associated with either a node or a relationship. The default indexing service in Neo4j is provided by Lucene, which is an Apache project that is designed for high-performance text-search-based projects. The component in Neo4j that provides this service is known as neo4j-lucene-index and comes packaged with the default distribution of Neo4j. You can browse its features and properties at http://repo1.maven.org/maven2/org/neo4j/neo4j-lucene-index/. We will look at some basic indexing operations through the Java API of Neo4j.

Creating an index makes use of the `IndexManager` class using the `GraphDatabaseService` object. For a graph with games and players as nodes and playing or waiting as the relationships, the following operations occur:

```
//Create the index reference
IndexManager idx = graphDb.index();
//Index the nodes
Index<Node> players = idx.forNodes( "players" );
Index<Node> games = idx.forNodes( "games" );
//Index the relationships in the graph
RelationshipIndex played = idx.forRelationships( "played" );
```

For an existing graph, you can verify that an entity has been indexed:

```
IndexManager idx = graphDb.index();
boolean hasIndexing = idx.existsForNodes( "players" );
```

To add an entity to an index service, we use the `add(entity_name)` method, and then for complete removal of the entity from the index, we use the `remove ("entity name")` method. In general, indexes cannot be modified on the fly. When you need to change an index, you will need to get rid of the current index and create a new one:

```
IndexHits<Node> result = players.get( "name", "Ronaldo" );
Node data = result.getSingle();
```

The preceding lines are used to retrieve the nodes associated with a particular index. In this case, we get an iterator for all nodes indexed as players who have the name `Ronaldo`. Indexes in Neo4j are useful to optimize the queries. Several visual wrappers have been developed to view the index parameters and monitor their performance. One such tool is Luke, which you can view at `https://code.google.com/p/luke/`.

Having told Neo4j we want to auto-index relationships and nodes, you might expect it to be able to start searching nodes straightaway, but in fact, this is not the case. Simply switching on auto-indexing doesn't cause anything to actually happen. Some people find that counterintuitive and expect Neo4j to start indexing all node and relationship properties straight away. In larger datasets, indexing everything might not be practical since you are potentially increasing storage requirements by a factor of two or more with every value stored in the Neo4j storage as well as the index. Clearly, there will also be a performance overhead on every mutating operation from the extra work of maintaining the index. Hence, Neo4j takes a more selective approach to indexing, even with auto-indexing turned on; Neo4j will only maintain an index of node or relationship properties it is told to index. The strategy here is simple and relies on the key of the property. Using the config map programmatically requires the addition of two properties that contain a list of key names to index as shown below.

Schema-based indexing

Since Neo4j 2.0, there is extended support for indexing on graph data, based on the labels that are assigned to them. Labels are a way of grouping together one or more entities (both nodes and relationships) under a single name. Schema indexed refers to the process of automatically indexing the labeled entities based on some property or a combination of properties of those entities. Cypher integrates well with these new features to locate the starting point of a query easily.

To create a schema-based index on the `name_of_player` property for all nodes with the label, you can use the following Cypher query:

```
CREATE INDEX ON :Player(name_of_player)
```

When you run such a query on a large graph, you can compare the trace of the path that Neo4j follows to reach the starting node of the query with and without indexing enabled. This can be done by sending the query to the Neo4j endpoint in your database machine in a `curl` request with the profile flag set to `true` so that the trace is displayed.

```
curl http://localhost:7474/db/data/cypher?profile=true -H "Accept:
application/json" -X POST -H "Content-type: application/json" --data
'{"query" : "match pl:Player where pl.name_of_player! = \"Ronaldo\"
return pl.name_of_player, pl.country"}'
```

The result that is returned from this will be in the form of a JSON object with a record of how the execution of the query took place along with the `_db_hits` parameter that tells us how many entities in the graph were encountered in the process.

The performance of the queries will be optimized only if the most-used properties in your queries are all indexed. Otherwise, Neo4j will have no utility for the indexing if it has one property indexed and the retrieval of another property match requires traversing all nodes. You can aggregate the properties to be used in searches into a single property and index it separately for improved performance. Also, when multiple properties are indexed and you want the index only on a particular property to be used, you can specify this using the following construct using the `p:Player(name_of_player)` index with schema indexes; we no longer have to specify the use of the index explicitly. If an index exists, it will be used to process the query. Otherwise, it will scan the whole domain. Constraints can be used with similar intent as the schema indexes. For example, the following query asserts that the `name_of_player` property in the nodes labeled as `Player` is unique:

```
CREATE CONSTRAINT ON (pl:Player) ASSERT player.name_of_player IS
UNIQUE
```

Currently, schema indexes do not support the indexing of multiple properties of the label under a same index. You can, however, use multiple indexes on different properties of nodes under the same label.

Indexing takes up space in the database, so when you feel an index is no longer needed, it is good to relieve the database of the burden of such indexes. You can remove the index from all labeled nodes using the DROP INDEX clause:

```
DROP INDEX ON :Player(name_of_player)
```

The use of schema indices is much simpler in comparison to manual or auto-indexing, and this gives an equally efficient performance boost to transactions and operations.

Indexing benefits and trade-offs

Indexing does not come for free. Since the underlying application code is responsible for the management and use of indexes, the strategy that is followed should be thought over carefully. Inappropriate decisions or flaws in indexing result in decreased performance or unnecessary use of disk storage space.

High on the list of trade-offs for indexing is the fact that an index result uses storage, that is, the higher the number of entities that are indexed, the greater the disk usage. Creating indexes for the data is basically the process of creating small lookup maps or tables to allow rapid access to the data in the graph. So, for write operations such as INSERT or UPDATE, we write the data twice, once for the creation of the node and then to write it to the index mapping, which stores a pointer to the created node.

Moreover, with an elevated number of indexes, operations for insertions and updates will take a considerable amount of time since nearly as many operations are performed to index as compared to creating or updating entities. The code base will naturally scale since updates/inserts will now require the modification of the index for that entity and as is observed, if you profile the time of your query, the time to insert a node with indexes is roughly twice of that when inserted without indexes.

On the other hand, the benefit of indexing is that query performance is considerably improved since large sections of the graph are eliminated from the search domain.

Note that storing the Neo4j-generated IDs externally in order to enable fast lookup is not a good practice, since the IDs are subject to alterations. The ID of nodes and relationships is an internal representation method, and using them explicitly might lead to broken processes.

Therefore, the indexing scenario would be different for different applications. Those that require updation or creation more frequently than reading operations should be light in indexing entities, whereas applications dealing primarily with reads should generously use indexes to optimize performance.

Migration techniques for SQL users

Neo4j has been around for just a few years, while most organizations that are trying to move into business intelligence and analytics have their decades of data piled up in SQL databases. So, rather than moving or transforming the data, it is better to fit in a graph database along with the existing one in order to make the process a less disruptive one.

Handling dual data stores

The two databases in our system are arranged in a way that the already-in-place MySQL database will continue being the primary mode of storage. Neo4j acts as the secondary storage and works on small related subsets of data. This would be done in two specific ways:

- Online mode for transactions that are critical for essential business decisions that are needed in real time and are operated on current sets of data
- The system can also operate in batch mode in which we collect the required data and process it when feasible

This will require us to first tune our Neo4j system to get updated with the historical data already present in the primary database system and then adapt the system to sync between the two data stores.

We will try to avoid data export between the two data stores and design the system without making assumptions about the underlying data model.

Analyzing the model

Let's use a simple entity set of people buying cars sold by dealers to illustrate the process. You can fit in the process to your existing data setup. We outline the features of the objects in our domains as follows:

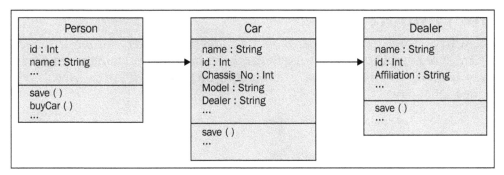

The SQL schema of an existing database

We can represent the corresponding model in Neo4j as a directed acyclic graph. The corresponding Neo4j acyclic graph handles the persistence with the database. Mutating Cypher is used to transform the data into a graph that contains nodes and relationships using the API of Neo4j in certain cases so that complex objects can be handled. Each entity relates back to the underlying database with the help of an ID that acts as the system's primary key and indexing operations are performed on this key. The corresponding graph model is as follows:

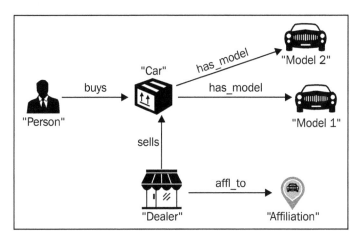

The corresponding representation in a graph database

When the graph modeling is complete, our application becomes independent of our primary data store.

Initial import

We now have to initiate the import of our data and store it after transformation into the form of our graph objects. We use SQL queries in order to obtain the required data by reading from the database, or requesting an existing API or previously exported set of data.

```
//Update a person node or create one. If created, its id is indexed.

SELECT name, id from person where
Person person=new Person(res.getString("name"), res.getInt("id"));
person.save();

//Update a car or create one. If created, its id is indexed.

SELECT name, id from car where
Car car=new Car(res.getString("name"),res.getInt("id"));
car.save();

//Update a dealer or create one. An "affiliation" node is created if
not already existing. A relationship is created to the affiliation
from the dealer. The ids of both dealer and affiliation are indexed.

SELECT name, id, affiliation from dealers where
Dealer dealer=new Dealer(res.getString("name"), res.getInt("id"));
dealer.setAffiliation(res.getString("affiliation"));
dealer.save();

//A relationship is created to the car from the person and we set the
date of buying as a property of that relationship

SELECT person.id, car.id, buying_date from Purchase_Table
Person person=repository.getById(res.getInt("customer.id"));
person.buyCar(res.getInt("id"),res.getDate("buying_date"));
```

Note that the preceding queries are abstract and will not run standalone. They illustrate the method of integrating with a relational database. You can change them according to your relational database schema.

Keeping data in sync

Having successfully imported data between the systems, we are now required to keep them in sync. For this purpose, we can schedule a cron job that will perform the previous operations in a periodic manner. You can also define an event-based trigger that will report on updates, such as cars being bought or new customers joining, in the primary system and incorporate them in the Neo4j application.

This can be implemented with simple concepts, such as message queues, where you can define the type of message required to be used by our secondary database system. Regardless of the content of the message, our system should be able to read and parse the message and use it for our business application logic.

The result

There is a loose coupling between the applications and we have used an efficient parsing approach to adapt the data between multiple formats. Although this technique works well for most situations, the import process might require a slightly longer time initially due to the transactional nature, but the initial import is not a process that occurs frequently. The sync based on events is a better approach in terms of performance.

You need an in-depth understanding of the data pattern in your application so that you can decide which technique is suitable. For single-time migrations of large datasets, there are several available tools such as the batch importer (`https://github.com/jexp/batch-import`) or the REST batch API on a database server that runs Neo4j.

Useful code snippets

Data storage and operations on data are essentially well framed and documented for Neo4j. When it comes to the analysis of data, it is much easier for the data scientists to get the data out of the database in a raw format, such as CSV and JSON, so that it can be viewed and analyzed in batches or as a whole.

Importing data to Neo4j

Cypher can be used to create graphs or include data in your existing graphs from common data formats such as CSV. Cypher uses the `LOAD CSV` command to parse CSV data into the form that can be incorporated in a Neo4j graph. In this section, we demonstrate this functionality with the help of an example.

We have three CSV files: one contains players, the second has a list of games, and the third has a list of which of these players played in each game. You can access the CSV files by keeping them on the Neo4j server and using `file://`, or by using FTP, HTTP, or HTTPS for remote access to the data.

Let's consider sample data about cricketers (players) and the matches (games) that were played by them. Your CSV file would look like this:

```
id,name
1,Adam Gilchrist
2,Sachin Tendulkar
3,Jonty Rhodes
4,Don Bradman
5,Brian Lara
```

You can now load the CSV data into Neo4j and create nodes out of them using the following commands, where the headers are treated as the labels of the nodes and the data from every line is treated as nodes:

```
LOAD CSV WITH HEADERS FROM "http://192.168.0.1/data/players.csv" AS
LineOfCsv
CREATE (p:Person { id: toInt(LineOfCsv.id), name: LineOfCsv.name })
```

Now, let's load the `games.csv` file. The format of the game data will be in the following format where each line would have the ID, the name of the game, the country it was played in, and the year of the game:

```
id,game,nation,year
1,Ashes,Australia,1987
2,Asia Cup,India,1999
3,World Cup,London,2000
```

The query to import the data would now also have the code to create a country node and relate the game with that country:

```
LOAD CSV WITH HEADERS FROM " http://192.168.0.1/data/games.csv" AS
LineOfCsv
MERGE (nation:Nation { name: LineOfCsv.nation })
CREATE (game:Game { id: toInt(LineOfCsv.id), game: LineOfCsv.game,
year:toInt(LineOfCsv.year) })
CREATE (game)-[:PLAYED_IN]->(nation)
```

Now, we go for importing the relationship data between the players and the games to complete the graph. The association would be many to many in nature since a game is related to many players and a player has played in many games; hence, the relationship data is stored separately. The user-defined field id in players and games needs to be unique for faster access while relating and also to avoid conflicts due to common IDs in the two sets. Hence, we index the ID fields from both the previous imports:

```
CREATE CONSTRAINT ON (person:Person) ASSERT person.id IS UNIQUE
CREATE CONSTRAINT ON (movie:Movie) ASSERT movie.id IS UNIQUE
```

To import the relationships, we read a line from the CSV file, find the IDs in players and games, and create a relationship between them:

```
USING PERIODIC COMMIT
LOAD CSV WITH HEADERS FROM "http://path/to/your/csv/file.csv" AS
csvLine

MATCH (player:Player { id: toInt(csvLine.playerId)}), (game:Game { id:
toInt(csvLine.movieId)})
CREATE (player)-[:PLAYED {role: csvLine.role }]->(game)
```

The CSV file that is to be used for snippets such as the previous one will vary according to the dataset and operations at hand, a basic version of which is represented here:

```
playerId,gameId,role
1,1,Batsman
4,1,WicketKeeper
2,1,Batsman
4,2,Bowler
2,2,Bowler
5,3,All-Rounder
```

In the preceding query, the use of PERIODIC COMMIT indicates to the Neo4j system that the query can lead to the generation of inordinate amounts of transaction states and therefore would require to be committed periodically to the database instead of once at the end. Your graph is now ready. To improve efficiency, you can remove the indexing from the id fields and also the field themselves the nodes since they were only needed for the creation of the graph.

Exporting data from Neo4j

Inherently, Neo4j has no direct format to export data. For the purpose of relocation or backup, the Neo4j database as a `.db` file can be stored, which is located under the DATA directory of your Neo4j base installation directory.

Cypher query results are returned in the form of JSON documents, and we can directly export the `json` documents by using curl to query Neo4j with Cypher. A sample query format is as follows:

```
curl -o output.json -H accept:application/json -H content-
type:application/json --data '{"query" : "your_query_here" }'
http://127.0.0.1:7474/db/data/cypher
```

You can also use the structr graph application platform (`http://structr.org`) to export data in the CSV format. The following curl format is used to export all the nodes in the graph:

```
curl http://127.0.0.1:7474/structr/csv/node_interfaces/export
```

To export relationships using the structr interface, the following commands are used:

```
curl http://127.0.0.1:7474/structr/csv/node_interfaces/out
```

```
curl http://127.0.0.1:7474/structr/csv/node_interfaces/in
```

These store the incoming and outgoing relationships in the graph. Although the two sets of results overlap, this is necessary with respect to nodes in order to retrieve the graph. A lot more can be done with structr other than exporting data, which you can find at its official website. Apart from the previously mentioned techniques, you can always use the Java API for retrieval by reading the data by entity, transforming it into your required format (CSV/JSON), and writing it to a file.

Summary

In this chapter, you learned about Cypher queries, the clauses that give Cypher its inherent power, and how to optimize your queries and data model in order to make the query engine robust. We saw the best practices for improved performance using the types of indexing we can use on our data including manual, auto, and schema-based indexing practices.

In the next chapter, we will look at graph models and schema design patterns while working with Neo4j.

3
Efficient Data Modeling with Graphs

Databases are not dumps for data; rather, they are planned and strategically organized stores that befit a particular objective. This is where modeling comes into the picture. Modeling is motivated by a specific need or goal so that specific facets of the available information are aggregated together into a form that facilitates structuring and manipulation. The world cannot be represented in the way it actually is; rather, simplified abstractions can be formed in accordance with some particular goal. The same is true for graph data representations that are close logical representations of the physical-world objects. Systems managing relational data have storage structures far different from those that represent data close to natural language. Transforming the data in such cases can lead to semantic dissonance between how we conceptualize the real world and data storage structure. This issue is, however, overcome by graph databases. In this chapter, we will look at how we can efficiently model data for graphs. The topics to be covered in this chapter are:

- Data models and property graphs
- Neo4j design constraints
- Techniques for modeling graphs
- Designing schemas
- Modeling across multiple domains
- Data models

Data models

A data model tells us how the logical structure of a database is modeled. Data models are fundamental entities to introduce abstraction in DBMS. They define how data is connected to each other and how it will be processed and stored inside the system. There are two basic types of data models in which related data can be modeled: **aggregated** and **connected**.

The aggregated data model

Aggregated data is about how you might use aggregation in your model to simulate relationships when you can't explicitly define them. So, you might store different objects internally in separate sections of the data store and derive the relationships on the fly with the help of foreign keys, or any related fields between the object. Hence, you are aggregating data from different sources, for example, as depicted in the following diagram, a company might contain a collection of the people who work there, and a person might in turn be associated with several products within the company, from which you might extract the related data. The aggregation or grouping is used to form a link between entities rather than a well-defined relationship.

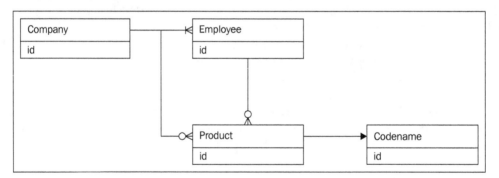

Connected data models

Connected data is about relationships that exist between different entities. We explicitly specify how the two entities are connected with a well-defined relationship and also the features of this relation, so we do not need to derive relationships. This makes data access faster and makes this the prominent data model for most graph databases, including Neo4j. An example would be a PLAYS_FOR relationship between a player and a team, as shown in the following diagram:

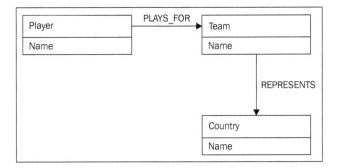

Property graphs

The graph structure that most graph databases including Neo4j use inherently classifies them into property graphs. A property graph stores the data in the form of nodes. These nodes are linked with relationships that provide structure to the graph. Relationships must have a direction and a label and must exist between a start node and an end node (dangling relationships are not permitted). Both nodes and relationships can have properties, which are key-value pairs that store characteristic information about that entity. The keys have to be strings that describe the property, while the value can be of any type. In property graphs, the number and type of properties can vary across the entities. You can basically store all the metadata about that entity into it in the form of properties. They are also useful in applying constraints to the queries for faster access with the help of indexes.

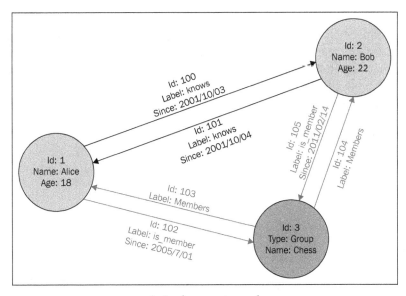

A simple property graph

These are all that are required to create the most sophisticated and rich semantic models for the graphs. Diagrams are an excellent way to view and design graph structure models since they clarify the data model. However, in order to implement these models in the Neo4j graph systems, you will need tools such as Cypher that provide elegant constructs to design the most complex of systems, some of which we will see later in the chapter.

Design constraints in Neo4j

Neo4j is very versatile in terms of data structuring, but everything has its limitations. So, a designer ought to know where Neo4j gives up so that he can weigh his data size and type and boil down to an efficient data model.

Size of files: Neo4j is based on Java at its core, so its file handling is dependent upon the nonblocking input/output system. Although there are several optimizations for interconnected data in the layout of storage files, there are no requirements of raw devices in Neo4j. Hence, the limitation on the file sizes is determined by the core operating system's ability to handle large files. There is no such built-in limit that makes it adaptable to big data scenarios. There is, however, a process of internal memory-mapping of the underlying file storage to the maximum extent. The beauty also lies in the fact that in systems where memory gradually becomes a constraint and the system is unable to keep all data in memory, Neo4j will make use of buffers that will dynamically reallocate the memory-mapped input/output windows to memory areas where most activity takes place. This helps to maintain the speed of ACID interactions.

Data read speed: Most organizations scale and optimize their hardware to deliver higher business value from already-existing resources. Neo4j's techniques of data reads provide efficient use of all available system hardware. In Neo4j, there is no blockage or locking of any read operation; hence, deadlocks need not be worried about and transactions are not required for reads. Neo4j implements a threaded access to the database for reads, so you can run simultaneous queries to the extent supported by your underlying system and on all available processors. For larger servers, this provides great scale-up options.

Data write speeds: Optimizing the write speed is something most organizations worry about. Writes occur in two different scenarios:

- Write in a continuous track in a sustained way
- Bulk write operations for initial data loads, batch processes, or backups

In order to facilitate writes in both these scenarios, Neo4j inherently has two modes of writing to the underlying layer of storage. In the normal ACID transactional operations, it maintains isolation, that is, reads can occur in the duration of the write process. When the commit is executed, Neo4j persists the data to the disk, and if the system fails, a recovery to the consistent state can be obtained. This requires access for writes to the disk and the data to be flushed to the disk. Hence, the limitation for writes on each machine is the I/O speed of the bus. In the case of deployment to production scenarios, high-speed flash SSDs are the recommended storage devices, and yes, Neo4j is flash ready.

Neo4j also comes with a **batch inserter** that can be used to directly work on the stored data files. This mode does not guarantee security for transactions, so they cannot be used in a multithreaded write scenario. The write process is sequential in nature on a single write thread without flushing to logs; hence, the system has great boosts to performance. The batch inserter is handy for the import of large datasets in nontransactional scenarios.

Size of data: For data in Neo4j, the limitation is the size of the address space for all the keys used as primary keys in lookup for nodes, relationships, and their properties and types. The address space at present is as follows:

Entity	Address space size
Nodes	235 (about 34 billion)
Relationships	235 (about 34 billion)
Relationship types	215 (about 32,000)
Properties	236 to 238 according to the type of the property (up to about 274 billion, but will always be a minimum of about 68 billion)

Security: There might arise scenarios where unauthorized access to the data in terms of modification and theft needs to be prevented. Neo4j has no explicitly supported data encryption methods but can use Java's core encryption constructs to secure the data before storing in the system. Security can also be ensured at the level of the file system using an encrypted data storage layer. Hence, security should be ensured at all levels of the hosted system to avoid malicious read-writes, data corruption, and **Distributed denial of service (DDOS)** attacks.

Graph modeling techniques

Graph databases including Neo4j are versatile pieces of software that can be used to model and store almost any form of data including ones that would be traditionally stored in RDBMS or document databases. Neo4j in particular is designed to have capabilities as a high-performance store for day-to-day transactional data as well as being usable for some level of analytics. Almost all domains including social, medical, and finance bring up problems that can easily be handled by modeling data in the form of graphs.

Aggregation in graphs

Aggregation is the process in which we can model trees or any other arbitrary graph structures with the help of denormalization into a single record or document entity.

- The maximum efficiency in this technique is achieved when the tree to be aggregated is to be accessed in a single read (for example, a complete hierarchy of comments of a post is to be read when the page with the post is loaded)

- Random accesses to the entries or searching on them can cause problems

- Aggregated nodes can lead to inefficient updates in contrast with independent nodes

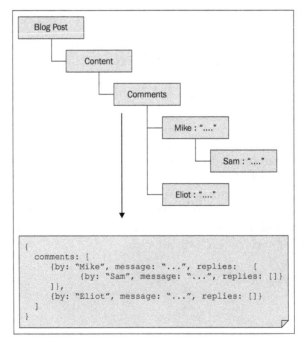

Aggregation of entities in a blog post tree

Graphs for adjacency lists

The simplest method of graph modeling is adjacency lists where every node can be modeled in the form of isolated records containing arrays with immediate descendants or ancestors. It facilitates the searching of nodes with the help of the identifiers and keys of their parents or ancestors and also graph traversal by pursuing hops for each query. This technique is, however, usually inefficient for retrieving complete trees for any given node and for depth- or breadth-based traversals.

Materialized paths

Traversal of tree-like hierarchical structures can sometimes lead to recursive traversals. These can be avoided with the help of materialized paths that are considered as a form of denormalization technique. We make the identifying keys of the node's parents and children as attributes or properties of the node. In this way, we minimize traversals by direct reference to the predecessors and descendants.

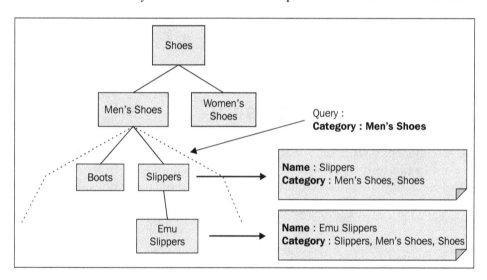

Since the technique allows the conversion of graph-like structures into flat documents, we can use it for full text-based searches. In the previous data scenario, the product list or even the subcategories can be retrieved using the category name in the query.

You can store materialized paths in the form of an ID set, or you can concatenate the IDs into a single string. Storing as a string allows us to make use of regular expressions to search the nodes for complete or partial criteria. This is shown in the following diagram (the node is included in the path):

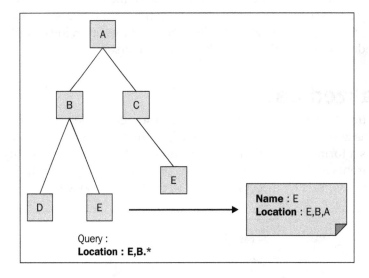

Modeling with nested sets

We can also use model-graph-based structures with the help of nested sets. Although it is used consistently with relational database systems, it is also applicable to NoSQL data stores. In this technique, we store the leaf nodes in the tree in the form of an array and then map the intermediate nodes to a range of child nodes using the initial and final indexes. This is illustrated in the following diagram:

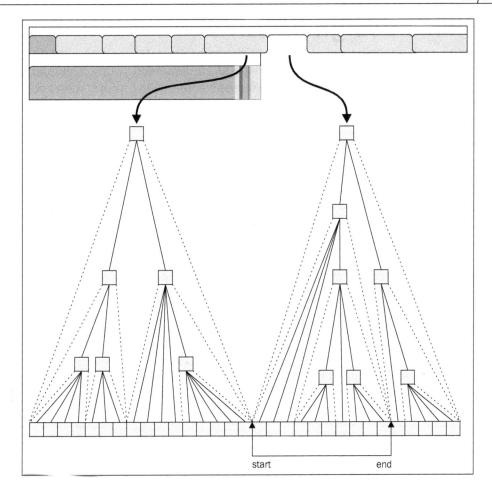

In due course, for data that is not modified, this structure will prove to be quite efficient since it takes up comparatively small memory and it fetches all the leaf nodes without traversals. On frequently changing data, it is not as effective since insertions and updation lead to extensive index updates and therefore is a costly affair.

Flattening with ordered field names

The operation of search engines is based on flattened documents of fields and values. In datasets for such applications, the goal of modeling is to map existing entities to plain documents or unified nodes that can be challenging when the structure of the graph is complex. We can combine multiple related nodes or relationships into single entities based on their use. For example, you can combine nodes. This technique is not really scalable since the complexity of the query is seen to grow quite rapidly as a function of a count of the structures that are combined.

Schema design patterns

Designing a schema will vary according to the scenario of data and operations that are being used. So, once you have designed and implemented your graph model, you need to use the appropriate schema to retrieve interesting information and patterns from the graph. The tool of preference would be Cypher, as it is essentially built around graphs. Let's look at some design scenarios.

Hyper edges

The data entities can have different levels of classifications, for example, different groups contain a given user, with different roles for each group and a user being part of several groups. The user can take up various roles in multiple groups apart from the one they are a member of. The association that exists between the user, their groups, and the roles can be depicted with the help of a hyper edge. This can be implemented in a property graph model with the help of a node that captures an n-ary relationship.

In mathematics, a hypergraph is a generalization of a graph in which an edge can connect any number of vertices. One edge that contains an arbitrary number of nodes is a hyper edge. Property graphs cannot natively support hyper edges. If you need a hyper edge in your model, then this can be simulated by introducing an extra node.

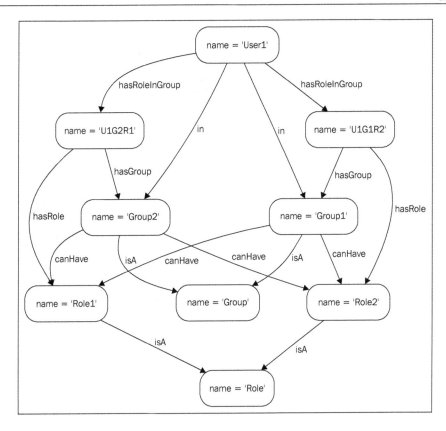

In order to compute a user's role in a certain group (**Group2** in this case), we make use of the following Cypher query for the traversal of the node with `HyperEdge` and calculate the results:

```
MATCH ({ name: 'User1' })-[:hasRoleInGroup]->(hyperEdge)-
[:hasGroup]->({ name: 'Group2' }),(hyperEdge)-[:hasRole]->(role)
RETURN role.name
```

The result returns the role of `User1` as `Role1`.

To calculate all the roles of a given user in the groups and display them in the form of an alphabetically sorted table, we need the traversal of the node with the HyperEdge:

```
MATCH ({ name: 'User1' })-[:hasRoleInGroup]->(hyperEdge)-[:hasGroup]-
>(group),(hyperEdge)-[:hasRole]->(role)
RETURN role.name, group.name
ORDER BY role.name ASC
```

The preceding query generates the following results:

role.name	group.name
"Role1"	"Group2"
"Role2"	"Group1"

Implementing linked lists

Since a graph database inherently stores data as a graph, it becomes an increasingly powerful tool to implement graph-based data structures such as linked lists and trees. For a linked list, we require the head or start node as the reference of the list. This node will have an outbound relation with the first element in the list and an inbound relation from the last element in the list. For an empty list, the reference points to itself. Such a linked list is called a circular list.

Let's initialize a linked list with no elements for which we first create a node that references itself. This is the start node used for reference; hence, it does not set a value as its property:

```
CREATE (start {name: 'START'})-[:POINTS]->(start)
RETURN start
```

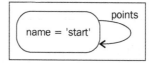

In order to add a value to it, we need to first find the relationship in which the new value should be placed. In this spot, in the place of the existing relationship, we add a new connecting node with two relationships to nodes on either ends. You also need to keep in mind that the nodes on either end can be the start node, which is the case when the list has no elements. To avoid the creation of two new value nodes, we are required to use the UNIQUE clause with the CREATE command. This can be illustrated with a Cypher query as follows:

```
MATCH (start)-[:POINTS*0..]->(prev),(next)-[:POINTS*0..]-
>(start),(prev)-[old:POINTS]->(next)
WHERE start.name = 'START' AND (prev.value < 25 OR next = start) AND
(25 < next.value OR next =
  start)
CREATE UNIQUE (prev)-[:POINTS]->({ value:25 })-[:POINTS]->(next)
DELETE old
```

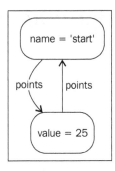

What this clause does is that it looks for the appropriate position of the value **25** in the list and replaces that relationship with a node containing 25 connected with two new relationships.

Complex similarity computations

When you have a heavily populated graph, you can perform numerous complex computations on it and derive interesting relations in large datasets of financial organizations, stock market data, social network data, or even sports data. For example, consider finding the similarity between two players based on the frequency with which they have been eating certain food (weird, huh!):

```
MATCH (roger { name: 'roger' })-[rel1:EATS]->(food)<-[rel2:EATS]-
(raphael)
WITH roger,count(DISTINCT rel1) AS H1,count(DISTINCT rel2) AS
H2,raphael
MATCH (roger)-[rel1:EATS]->(food)<-[rel2:EATS]-(raphael)
RETURN sum((1-ABS(rel1.times/H1-rel2.times/H2))*(rel1.times+rel2.
times)/(H1+H2)) AS similarity
```

Hence, complex computations can be carried out with minimal code involvement.

Route generation algorithms

The greatest advantage of having your data in the form of a graph is that you generate custom paths based on your requirements. For example, you need to find the common friend of two people; what you essentially have to do is find the shortest paths of length 2 using the two users and the connecting relationship between the entities. This will give us the users who are connected to the given people by a friend hop count of 1. Neo4j has a few graph de facto algorithms including those for the shortest path, which can be used in the following format:

```
PathFinder<Path> PathToFind = GraphAlgoFactory.shortestPath(
        Traversal.expanderForTypes( FRNDS_WITH ), 2 );
Iterable<Path> CommonPaths = PathToFind.findAllPaths( person1, person2
);
```

If Cypher is what appeals to you, then to return mutual friends of person1 and person2 by using traversals of the graph, you need the following snippet:

```
start person1 = node(3),person2 = node(24) match (person1)--
(Relation)--(person2) return Relation;
```

If you are interested in getting all the friends of a given person person1, then all you need to do is this:

```
start person1 = node(3) match person1--relation--person2 where
person1--person2 return relation;
```

Let's look at a code snippet that uses Neo4j's existing traversal algorithms on a graph modeled with weighted edges to calculate the least total weight (call this distance for now):

```
import org.neo4j.graphdb.Node;
import org.neo4j.kernel.Traversal;
import org.neo4j.graphalgo.PathFinder;
import org.neo4j.graphalgo.CostEvaluator;
import org.neo4j.graphdb.Direction;
import org.neo4j.graphalgo.WeightedPath;
import org.neo4j.graphalgo.GraphAlgoFactory;
import org.neo4j.graphalgo.CommonEvaluators;
import org.neo4j.graphdb.RelationshipExpander;
/**
 * Finding shortest path (least weighted) in a graph
 */
public class DijkstraPath
{
    private final GraphServiceHelper graph;
```

```java
//Included in the code folder
private static final String WEIGHT = "weight";
private static final CostEvaluator<Double> evalCost;
private static final PathFinder<WeightedPath> djktraFindPath;
private static final RelationshipExpander relExpndr;

static
{
    // configure the path finder
    evalCost = CommonEvaluators.doubleCostEvaluator( WEIGHT );
    relExpndr = Traversal.expanderForTypes(GraphServiceHelper.
MyDijkstraTypes.REL, Direction.BOTH );
    djktraFindPath = GraphAlgoFactory.dijkstra( relExpndr,
evalCost );
}

public DijkstraPath()
{
    graph = new GraphServiceHelper( "path_to_database" );
}

private void constructGraph()
{
    graph.createRelationship( "n1", "n2", WEIGHT, 10d );
    graph.createRelationship( "n2", "n5", WEIGHT, 10d );
    graph.createRelationship( "n1", "n3", WEIGHT, 5d );
    graph.createRelationship( "n3", "n4", WEIGHT, 10d );
    graph.createRelationship( "n4", "n5", WEIGHT, 5d );
}

/**
 * Find the path.
 */
private void executeDijkstraFindPath()
{
    Node begin = graph.getNode( "n1" );
    Node endd = graph.getNode( "n5" );
    WeightedPath path = djktraFindPath.findSinglePath( begin, endd
);
    for ( Node node : path.nodes() )
    {
        System.out.println( node.getProperty( GraphServiceHelper.
NAME ) );
    }
}
```

```
/**
 * Shutdown the graphdb.
 */
private void stop()
{
    graph.shutdown();
}


/**
 * Execute the example.
 */
public static void main( final String[] args )
{
    DijkstraPath obj = new DijkstraPath();
    obj.constructGraph();
    obj.executeDijkstraFindPath();
    obj.stop();
}
}
```

Modeling across multiple domains

Most organizations use Neo4j for the purpose of business applications. Developers might sometimes argue that in designing the underlying data model, there ought to be multiple graphs that are classified on the basis of subdivided domains. Others might insist on having all of the data of the domain in a single large graph. If you consider the facts, both these scenarios have their own trade-offs.

If the subdivided domain datasets are queried frequently in such a way that the traversals are spread across multiple domains, then the developer who suggested a single large graph is right. However, if you are confident that the subdivided domains will rarely need to interact among themselves, then it would be effective to use the multiple small graphs. This will make the system more robust and decrease the query response time.

With all this said, it is important to outline that the more messy your graph looks with interconnections of all kinds, the more complex queries you can practically run to derive highly interesting relationships that will make your application more complex and intelligent. For example, if your comprehension of music was to be completely independent of your ability to play soccer, then the movements of the goalkeeper will not appear like dancing (if you are thinking of music while watching a match, you could actually interpret the movements as a dance). Humans on the other hand are capable of seamlessly mixing so many different variations.

Domains or subdomains for that matter are rarely different in the truest sense; they overlap at times, which can be a benefit for your app if the traversals can make use of explicit continuities in such cases. Performance depends on how frequently you traverse and the methods you use for it. The data size and density of related data are rather insignificant for performance if you decide to subdivide your graph into chunks.

Although it would not be a preferred choice on single machines, if you need to subdivide your graph based on domains, you need to keep in mind that Neo4j graphs are essentially directories in the filesystem. So, in order to link them, you would be required to create a class to dynamically load the path of the database needed into memory for the querying process and remove it when the result of the query is obtained. In a real-time scenario where loads of queries need to processed on the fly, this is not a good idea. However, for scenarios where you need to warehouse your data for analysis purposes, it definitely works well.

Insights for businesses require us to understand the underlying network actions in a complex chain of values. This might require us to perform joins across several domains with little or no distortion in the details of each domain. This process is simplified with property graphs, where we can model a chain of values as a forest (that is, a graph of graphs) that can include interdomain relationships on rare occasions.

Summary

Even though modeling graphs seems to be a quite expressive method of handling the level of complexity associated with a problem domain, this expressivity is not a guarantee that the graph is fit for the purpose it is designed for. There are several issues of wrong modeling among graph data users, but eventually, you learn which model is suitable for the scenario at hand.

In this chapter, we looked at how vivid modeling is possible when you have data in graphs. We also looked at how Neo4j data can be modeled with Cypher as a tool to decipher interesting relationships directly, which would otherwise require several hours of computation.

In the next chapter, we will look at scenarios that handle high-volume data in Neo4j applications.

4
Neo4j for High-volume Applications

There is an exponential surge in the amount of data being created annually; a pattern that is going to exist for quite some time. As data gets more complex, it is increasingly challenging to get valuable insights and information from it. However, the volume and complexity of data are not the only issues. There appears to be a rise in semi-structured and highly interconnected data. Several major tech firms such as Facebook, Google, and Twitter have resorted to the graph approach to tackle complexity in the big data arena. The analysis of trends and patterns out of the collected raw data has begun to gain popularity. From professional outlook websites such as LinkedIn to tiny specialized social media applications cropping up each day, all have a graph-processing layer in their core applications. The graph-oriented approach has led many industries to come up with scalable systems to manage information.

A multitude of next-generation databases that provide better performance and support for semi-structured data form the backbone of the big data revolution today. These technologies not only make the analysis, storage, and management of high volumes of data simpler, they also scale up and scale out at an extraordinary rate. Graph databases are crucial players that have made it convenient to house an information web in your application that can be traversed through labeled relationships. Graph problems are existent all round us—from managing access rights and permission in security systems to looking for where you put the keys and from simple graphs to complex social ones—a graph database can provide more natural storage and rapid querying.

In this chapter, we will look at the use of graphs and the Neo4j database in scenarios that handle large volumes of data including:

- Graph processing
- Use of graphs in big data
- Transaction management
- The `graphalgo` package of Neo4j
- Introducing spring data Neo4j

Graph processing

Graph processing is an exciting development for those in the graph database space, since the utility of graph databases has been reinforced as a storage system as well as a computational model. However, the processing of graph-like data can be confused with graph databases due to the common data models they share, although each technique operates on fundamentally different scenarios. Some graph-processing platforms such as Pregel, developed by Google, are capable of achieving high-computational throughput, since it adopts the **Bulk Synchronous Processing** (BSP) model from the domain of parallel computing. This model supports the partition of the graph into multiple machines and uses the localized data from the vertices for computation. Exchange of local information takes place during the synchronization process. This model is used to process large interconnected datasets for business insights compared to traditional map-reduce operations, although high latency is a concern in this case.

For enterprise scenarios, a popular batch-processing platform for large volumes of data is Hadoop. Similar to Pregel, Hadoop is also a high-throughput and latency system that is used to optimize throughputs of computation for extremely large datasets and that too in parallel and exterior to the database. However, Hadoop is made for general computational use and although you can use it for processing graphs, the system and the components are "un-optimized" for graph-oriented operations.

What the two platforms have in common is the efficient handling of **Online Analytical Processing** (OLAP) for analytics, rather than simply dealing with transactions. This is contrary to the principles of Neo4j and other graph databases. These principles prioritize the optimization of storage and queries for **Online Transaction Processing** (OLTP), similar to relational databases, but implement a more powerful, simple, and expressive underlying data model. This can visualized from the following diagram:

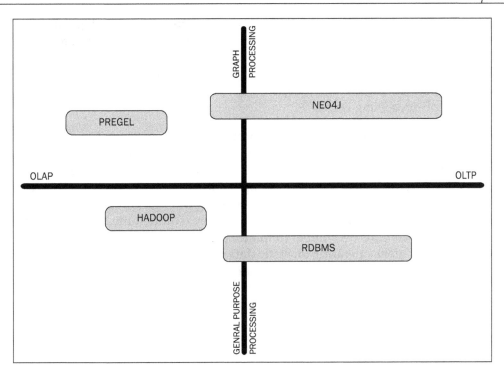

As depicted in the preceding diagram, Pregel is strictly an OLAP graph-processing tool; Hadoop is a completely general-purpose OLAP system but it is closer to the OLTP axis since several current extensions are available to achieve near real-time processing with Hadoop. Relational databases are mostly OLTP systems that can be logically adapted in systems that require OLAP processing. Neo4j is designed solely for graph data and primarily involves scenarios for OLTP operations, although it can also be used for OLAP since it has a native graph model and high-read capability.

Big data and graphs

Graph data analysis is a prime technique to extract information from very large datasets by assessing the similarity or associativity of data points. The need for such techniques arose when social networks started gaining popularity and expanded their user base rapidly, but today, graph analysis has a much broader scope of application.

Since graph processing has caught up in the race for crunching data, big data platforms and communities have been innovatively adapting themselves to the needs for solving graph problems with frameworks, such as Apache Giraph (`http://giraph.apache.org/`) and MapReduce extensions such as Pregel (`goo.gl/hW3L40`), Surfer, and GBASE (`http://goo.gl/3QkB46`); it is becoming simpler to address graph-processing issues.

Hadoop is a large-scale distributed batch-processing framework that operates at high latencies unlike graph databases. So, if you implement graph processing on a Hadoop-based system, data locality will lead to a more efficient batch execution, and therefore, we will see a higher throughput. However, latency still remains the drawback. Hence, the approach of graph processing through Hadoop batch jobs will not be feasible for OLTP applications, since they require quite low latency in the order of milliseconds (as compared to the seconds in Hadoop). Hence, it will find more applications operating on static data in the OLAP domain. You can use this for report generation purposes from static data stored in warehouses, especially if the data is carefully laid out. In order to increase the efficiency of such a system, denormalization of the data needs to take place within the HBase data store, which increases the cognitive difference between the obtained data and the manner in which it is represented for the purpose of graph processing.

However, Neo4j rules out these drawbacks. If you use Neo4j for the purposes of graph processing, you do not need to denormalize the data or set up any specialized infrastructure. Neo4j works seamlessly in OLTP and uses the same database (most often, a read-only replica in sync with the master) for OLAP, should you require to use it. The main advantage here is the low latency even when dealing with larger read queries as well as when exposed to heavy online loads.

Hadoop-based, batch-oriented graph processing is beneficial in scenarios where you can read or process data external to the database as compared to manipulating it in place. So, to obtain efficient processing, data needs to be carefully placed in HBase with no scope of mutation in the course of the processing. Neo4j, on the other hand, supports mutations of the graph in place, which is an essential feature to run analytics on real-time web data.

Processing with Hadoop or Neo4j

The Hadoop-based solution processes batches to provide high throughputs but at the cost of high latency and denormalization of data. The Neo4j approach is the perfect candidate for OLTP processing on native graph data, with an added advantage of real-time OLAP operations that provide a modest throughput but speed things up with a quite low latency. So, depending upon the type of data and the requirement of your application, you can select one of the methods for an advanced graph-processing approach. If OLTP is what you need with deep analytical insights into your data in near real-time, then Neo4j is the answer to your prayers. For more relaxed scenarios that can bear the high latencies in order to achieve higher throughput, then you should consider graph-processing platforms such as Hadoop or Pregel (developed at Google).

In fact, there have also been attempts to combine Hadoop's processing capabilities with the native graph storage of Neo4j. You can check this out at `http://goo.gl/OTgfML`.

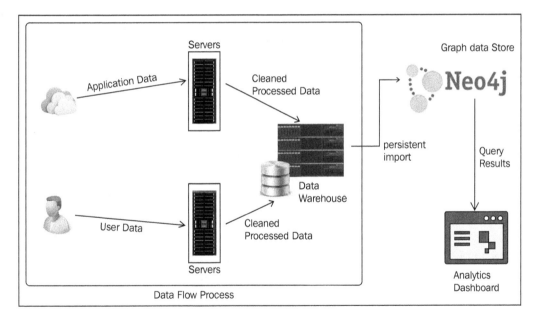

Neo4j performs best in an in-memory dataset that leads to blazing-fast traversals and implementations of complex logic. However, as the number of datasets increase, it becomes difficult to incorporate all of it in memory for processing. Also, distributing the dataset across multiple Neo4j instances is possible but decreases the traversal speed. So, an alternate approach needs to be found. Analytics of the data is not generally an online process. You can make use of this fact to intermittently load only that part of the data you would require for the current analytical transaction, process it, and then load new data for another. So, only when the need to populate the analytics dashboard field arises do you load and process the data in Neo4j. This process is illustrated in the preceding diagram. This technique is beneficial since the importing of data in Neo4j costs relatively less compared to the analytical processing of graphs in a relational or distributed data store.

Managing transactions

Consider corporate scenarios, or businesses generating tons of critical data; operating on them in real time is a responsibility. On one hand, there are corporations such as Twitter or IMDb where the volume of data is high but the criticality of data is not a top priority. However, on the other hand, there are firms that handle high volumes of connected financial or medical data, where maintaining the integrity of data is of the utmost importance. Such scenarios require ACID transactions, which most databases today have built-in support for. Neo4j is a fully ACID database, as we discussed in *Chapter 1, Getting Started with Neo4j*; it ensures the following properties with respect to transactions:

- **Atomicity**: When a part of the transaction is unsuccessful, the state of the database is not changed

- **Consistency**: The transaction maintains the database in a consistent state

- **Isolation**: When transactions take place, the data being operated upon is not accessible to any other process

- **Durability**: It is possible to roll back or recover the committed transaction results

Neo4j has provision to ensure that whenever graph access, indexing, or schema-altering operations take place, they must be processed in transactions. This is implemented with the help of locks. Neo4j allows nonrepeatable reads, in other words, the transactions acquire write-level locks that are only released when the transaction terminates. You can also acquire write locks manually on entities (nodes or relationships) for higher isolation levels such as SERIALIZABLE. The default level is READ_COMMITTED. The core API for a transaction also has provisions to handle deadlocks, which we will discuss later in the chapter.

A transaction is confined at the thread level. You also nest your transactions, where the nested transactions are part of the scope of the highest-level transaction. These transactions are referred to as *flat nested transactions*. In such transactions, when there is an exception in a nested transaction, the complete highest-level transaction needs to roll back, since alterations of a nested transaction alone cannot be rolled back.

The database constantly monitors the transaction state, which basically involves the following operations:

1. A transaction begins.
2. Operations are performed on the database.
3. Indicate whether the transaction was a success or a failure.
4. The transaction finishes.

The transaction must finish in order to release the acquired locks and the memory used. In Neo4j, we use a `try-finally` code segment where the transaction is started and the write operations are performed. The `try` block should end by marking the transaction successful and the transaction should be finished by the `finally` block, where the `commit` or `rollback` operation is performed depending upon the success status of the transaction. It is important to keep in mind that any alterations performed in a transaction are in memory, which is why for high-volume scenarios with frequent transactions, we need to divide the updates into multiple higher- or top-level transactions to prevent the shortage of memory:

```
Transaction tx = graphDb.beginTx();
try
{
    // operations on the graph
    // ...

    tx.success();
}
finally
{
    tx.close();
}
```

Since transactions operate with thread pools, other errors might be occurring when a transaction experiences a failure. When a transaction thread has not finished properly, it is not terminated and marked for `rollback` and will result in errors when a write operation is attempted for that transaction. When performing a read operation, the previous value committed will be read, unless the transaction that is currently being processed makes changes just before the read. By default, the level of isolation implemented is `READ_COMMITTED`, which means that no locks are imposed on read operations, and hence, the read operations can occur in a nonrepeatable fashion. If you manually specify the read and write locks to be used, then you can implement a higher level of isolation, namely, `SERIALIZABLE` or `REPEATABLE_READ`. Generally, write locks are implemented when you create, modify, or delete a particular entity as outlined in the following points:

- Writelock a node or relationship when you add, change, or remove properties.

- The creation and deletion of nodes and relationships require you to implement a write lock. For relationships, the two connecting nodes need to be write-locked as well.

Neo4j comes equipped with deadlock detection, where a deadlock occurring due to the locking arrangement can be detected before it happens and Neo4j churns out an exception to indicate the deadlock. Also, the transaction is flagged to be rolled back before the exception is thrown. When the locks held are released in the `finally` block, other transaction operations that were busy waiting on the resource can now take up the lock and proceed. However, the user can choose to retry the failed/deadlocked transaction at a later time.

Deadlock handling

When deadlocks occur frequently, it is generally an indication that the concurrent write requests are not possible to execute to maintain consistency and isolation. To avoid such scenarios, concurrent write updates must be executed in a reasonable fashion. For example, deadlocks can happen when we randomly create or delete relationships between the two given nodes. The solution is to always execute the updates in a specific order (first on node 1 and then on node 2 always) or by manually ensuring that there are no conflicting operations in the concurrent threads by confining similar types of operations to a single thread.

All tasks performed by the Neo4j API are thread-safe in nature, unless you explicitly specify otherwise. So, any other synchronized blocks in your code should not include operations relating to Neo4j. There is a special case that Neo4j includes while deleting nodes or relationships. If you try to delete a node or relationship completely, the properties will undergo deletion, while the relationships will be spared. What? Why? That's because Neo4j imposes a constraint on relationships that have valid start and end nodes. So, if you try to delete nodes that are still connected by relationships, an exception is raised on committing transactions. So, the transaction must be planned in such a way that no relationships to a node being deleted must exist when the current transaction is about to be committed. The semantic conventions that must be followed when a delete operation is required to be performed are summarized as follows:

- When you delete a node or relationship, all properties are deleted.
- Before committing, a node must not have relationships attached to it.
- A node or relationship is not actually deleted unless a commit takes place; hence, you can reference a deleted entity before commits. However, you cannot write to such a reference.

Uniqueness of entities

Duplication is another issue to deal with when multithreaded operations are in play. It is possible that there is only one player with a given name in the world, but transactions on concurrent threads trying to create such a node can end up creating duplicated entities. Such operations need to be prevented. One naïve approach would be to use a single thread to create the particular entities. Another popular approach that is used most often is to use the get_or_create operation. We can guarantee uniqueness with the help of indexing where legacy indices are used as locks for the smallest unique identity of the entity to enable creation only if the lookup for that particular entity fails. The other existing one is simply returned. This concept of get_or_create exists for Cypher as well as the Java API. This ensures uniqueness across all transactions and threads.

There is also a third technique called pessimistic locking that is implemented across common nodes or a single node, where a lock is manually created and used to check for synchronization. However, this approach does not apply to a high-availability scenario.

Events for transactions

Event handlers for transactions keep track of what happens in the course of a transaction before it goes for a commit. You need to register an event handler to an instance of the `GraphDatabaseService`, events can be received. Handlers are not notified if the transaction does not perform any writes or the transaction fails to commit. There are two methods, `beforeCommit` and `afterCommit`, that calculate the changes in the data (the difference) due to that commit and that constitutes an event.

Let's now see a simple example where a transaction is executed through the Java API to see how the components fit together:

```
public void transactionDemo() {

    GraphDatabaseService graphDatabase;
    Node node1;
    Node node2;
    Relationship rel;

    graphDatabase = new GraphDatabaseFactory().newEmbeddedDatabase(
DB_PATH );
    registerShutdownHook( graphDatabase );

    Transaction txn = graph.beginTx();
    try {
        node1 = graphDatabase.createNode();
        node1.setProperty( "name", "David Tennant" );
        node2 = graphDatabase.createNode();
        node2.setProperty( "name", "Matt Smith" );

        rel = node1.createRelationshipTo( node2, RelTypes.KNOWS );
        rel.setProperty( "name", "precedes " );

        node1.getSingleRelationship( RelTypes.KNOWS, Direction.
OUTGOING ).delete();
        node1.delete();
        node2.delete();

        txn.success();
    } catch (Exception e) {
        txn.failure();
    } finally {
        txn.finish();
    }
}
```

When you are using the Neo4j REST server or operating in the high-availability mode, then the following syntax can be used:

```
POST http://localhost:7474/db/data/transaction/commit
Accept: application/json; charset=UTF-8
Content-Type: application/json
{
  "statements" : [ {
    "statement" : "CREATE (n {props}) RETURN n",
    "parameters" : {
      "props" : {
        "name" : "My Node"
      }
    }
  } ]
}
```

The preceding REST request begins a transaction and commits it after completion. If you want to keep the transaction open for more requests, then you need to drop the commit option from the POST request as follows:

```
POST http://localhost:7474/db/data/transaction
```

Post this at the end of the transaction to commit:

```
POST http://localhost:7474/db/data/transaction/9/commit
```

Transactions are the core components that make Neo4j ACID-compliant and suitable for use in scenarios where high volumes of complex critical data are being used. Transactions, if managed efficiently, can make your application robust and consistent, even in scenarios that require real-time updates.

The graphalgo package

A graph provides a very attractive solution when you want to model real-world data. As they are more flexible than RDBMS, they offer an intuitive approach and are practically relevant to the way we think of stuff. The graph world revolves around several featured algorithms that are used to process graphs and for route calculation, detection of loops, calculation of the shortest path, subgraph and pattern matching being a few of them. Although you can implement your own collection of algorithms and tweaks, Neo4j also includes a set of predefined algorithms that you use most for rapid application development, even for scenarios that involve large volumes of data. They are packaged in a library called the `graphalgo` that you can use directly in your Java code fragments. The REST API also exposes a few of these algorithms such as dijkstra's and A* to be used with requests sent to the REST server. The `graphalgo` interfaces can be accessed and used in your programs using methods of the `GraphAlgoFactory` class. Some of the methods that can prove quite useful at times are:

- `allPaths(PathExpander, int)`: This method returns an algorithm that can be used to calculate all possible paths between two specified nodes. Paths with loops can also be calculated using this method.

- `allSimplePaths(PathExpander, int)`: This method returns an algorithm that does a similar job as the allPaths algorithm, except that it returns paths that do not contain a loop.

- `aStar(PathExpander, CostEvaluator<Double>, EstimateEvaluator<Double>)`: This method returns a variable of type `PathFinder` that can use the A* algorithm to calculate the path with the minimum weight/cost between two specified nodes.

- `dijkstra(PathExpander, CostEvaluator<Double>)`: This method returns a variable of type `PathFinder` that operates similar to the one in the previous method, except it uses the Dijkstra's algorithm instead of A*.

- `pathsWithLength(PathExpander, int)`: It returns an algorithm that can be used to a specific weighted path between two nodes.

- `shortestPath(PathExpander, int)`: From this method, you get an algorithm to calculate all possible shortest paths that exist between a given pair of nodes.

All the preceding algorithms use an instance of `PathExpander` as a parameter, which contains the logic to decide which relationship to expand on, or select the next relationship in the process of traversal. Alternatively, the preceding methods also allow the use of `RelationshipExpander`, which is a similarly flexible way of getting the relationships from a particular node. All the preceding methods return a value of the type `PathFinder`, which you can use to retrieve the paths from the algorithms. Let's see the use of some of these through an example:

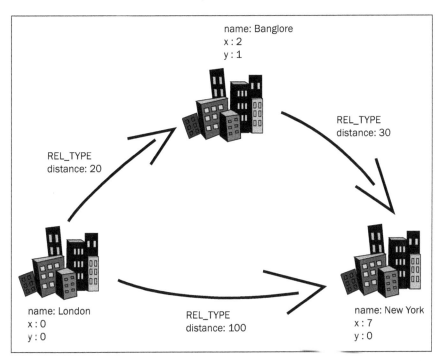

The preceding diagram illustrates a graphical scenario of interconnected cities that we will be using for our example. The following code shows how the graph can be created and operated upon:

```
//Create a sample graph
Node cityA = createNode( "city", "London", "x", 0d, "y", 0d );
Node cityB = createNode( "city", "New York", "x", 7d, "y", 0d );
Node cityC = createNode( "city", "Bangalore", "x", 2d, "y", 1d );
Relationship distAB = createRelationship( cityA, cityC, "distance",20d
);
Relationship distBC = createRelationship( cityC, cityB, "distance",30d
);
```

```
Relationship distAC = createRelationship( cityA, cityB,
"distance",100d );

EstimateEvaluator<Double> estimateEvaluator = new
EstimateEvaluator<Double>()
{
    @Override
    public Double getCost( final Node node, final Node goal )
    {
        double costx = (Double) node.getProperty( "x" ) - (Double)
goal.getProperty( "x" );
        double costy = (Double) node.getProperty( "y" ) - (Double)
goal.getProperty( "y" );
        double answer = Math.sqrt( Math.pow( costx, 2 ) + Math.pow(
costy, 2 ) );
        return answer;
    }
};


//Use the A* algorithm
PathFinder<WeightedPath> astarFinder = GraphAlgoFactory.
aStar(PathExpanders.allTypesAndDirections(),
    CommonEvaluators.doubleCostEvaluator( "distance" ),
estimateEvaluator );
WeightedPath astarPath = astarFinder.findSinglePath( cityA, cityB );


//Using the Dijkstra's algorithm
PathFinder<WeightedPath> dijkstraFinder = GraphAlgoFactory.dijkstra(
    PathExpanders.forTypeAndDirection( ExampleTypes.REL_TYPE,
Direction.BOTH ), "distance" );

WeightedPath shortestPath = dijkstraFinder.findSinglePath( cityA,
cityC );
//print the weight of this path
System.out.println(shortestPath.weight());


//Using the find all paths method
PathFinder<Path> allPathFinder = GraphAlgoFactory.shortestPath(
    PathExpanders.forTypeAndDirection( ExampleTypes.REL_TYPE,
Direction.OUTGOING ), 15 );
Iterable<Path> all_paths = allPathFinder.findAllPaths( cityA, cityC );
```

The REST interface of the Neo4j server is also capable of executing these graph algorithms, where you can define the start node and the type of algorithm in the body of the POST request, as illustrated here:

```
POST http://localhost:7474/db/data/node/264/path
Accept: application/json; charset=UTF-8
Content-Type: application/json
{
  "to" : "http://localhost:7474/db/data/node/261",
  "cost_property" : "cost",
  "relationships" : {
    "type" : "to",
    "direction" : "out"
  },
  "algorithm" : "dijkstra"
}
```

These algorithms operate efficiently in moderate to large graphs. However, when you are processing graphs that require visiting billions of vertices that are highly connected in the graph, you can tweak these algorithms to improve performance. For example, if your graph cannot fit on a single instance and you resort to a cluster, then you need to modify your algorithm to traverse across machines, or to calculate in parts. However, for most big data scenarios today, they provide optimal performance.

Introduction to Spring Data Neo4j

The Spring MVC web framework is a project that exposes a model-view-controller architecture along with components that can be used for the development of loosely coupled and highly flexible web-based applications. The MVC-based approach is useful for differentiating the various aspects of an application—the input and the business and UI logic—and provides a loosely coupled relation between the elements.

The Spring Data project was designed to ease the process of using relatively newer technologies, such as map-reduce jobs, nonrelational and schema-less databases, and cloud data services, to build Spring-powered applications. As far as graph databases are considered, this project currently has support for Neo4j integration.

Spring Data Neo4j is a project that exposes a simple **Plain Old Java Object (POJO)** model for developers to program with, which is useful in reducing the boilerplate code (code that sees inclusion in several places without much alteration) that goes into the creation of applications with Neo4j. This helps to extend the **Java Persistence API (JPA)** data model in order to provide a cross-store solution for persistence that uses new parts such as entities, properties, and relationships exclusively to handle graphs. However, it is integrated in a transparent manner with pre-existing JPA entities, which provides an edge over simple JPA-based applications. The Spring Data Neo4j framework also includes features to map the annotated entity classes with the underlying Neo4j graph database. It uses a template programming model that presents a similar approach to the Spring templates, and this accounts for the interactivity with graphs and also has repository support. The following are some of the salient features of this framework:

- It integrates well with property graphs and has support for Gremlin and Cypher
- Transparent access to the Neo4j server with the REST API can also be run as an extension to the Neo4j server
- It has dynamic field traversal support and also extensive indexing practices
- Object-graph mapping for Java object entities
- Support for Spring Data repositories and dynamic type projections

Let's take a look at how you can set up a Spring Data Neo4j project to build an application that runs Neo4j as a data store. Using a dependency management system such as Maven or Gradle is the recommended approach to setting up the project. To include the latest stable build of SDN in your project, specify the following dependency in your pom.xml file:

```
<dependency>
    <groupId>org.springframework.data</groupId>
    <artifactId>spring-data-Neo4j</artifactId>
    <version>3.2.0.RELEASE</version>
</dependency>
```

Alternatively, if you intend to use REST API calls to access the remote Neo4j server, then the SDN dependency for REST should be included:

```
<dependency>
    <groupId>org.springframework.data</groupId>
    <artifactId>spring-data-Neo4j-rest</artifactId>
    <version>2.0.0.RELEASE</version>
</dependency>
```

Similar to other Spring Data projects, you need to define the special XML namespaces in order to configure your project. We simply need to provide the interface methods to define the custom finders we need to implement, and at runtime, Spring injects the appropriate implementation at runtime. The following context can be used for configuration:

```
<beans xmlns="http://www.springframework.org/schema/beans"
       xmlns:context="http://www.springframework.org/schema/context"
       xmlns:xsi="http://www.w3.org/2001/XMLSchema-instance"
       xmlns:Neo4j="http://www.springframework.org/schema/data/Neo4j"
       xsi:schemaLocation="http://www.springframework.org/schema/beans
http://www.springframework.org/schema/beans/spring-beans-
3.0.xsd">http://www.springframework.org/schema/beans/spring-beans-
3.0.xsd
       http://www.springframework.org/schema/
context">http://www.springframework.org/schema/context
href="http://www.springframework.org/schema/context/spring-context-
3.0.xsd">http://www.springframework.org/schema/context/spring-context-
3.0.xsd
       http://www.springframework.org/schema/data/
Neo4j">http://www.springframework.org/schema/data/Neo4j
href="http://www.springframework.org/schema/data/Neo4j/spring-Neo4j.
xsd">http://www.springframework.org/schema/data/Neo4j/spring-Neo4j.
xsd">

    <context:spring-configured/>
    <context:annotation-config/>

    <Neo4j:config storeDirectory="target/data/db"/>

    <Neo4j:repositories base-package="com.comsysto.Neo4j.showcase"/>
</beans>
```

If you plan to use your Spring application to interface with the REST API, then you need to include the server URL to direct the calls, as shown in the following code:

```
<!-- REST Connection to Neo4j server -->
<bean id="restGraphDatabase" class="org.springframework.data.Neo4j.
rest.SpringRestGraphDatabase">
  <constructor-arg value="http://localhost:7474/db/data/" />
</bean>

<!-- Neo4j configuration (creates Neo4jTemplate) -->
<Neo4j:config graphDatabaseService="restGraphDatabase" />
```

Example

```
//Creating a node entity
@NodeEntity
class Player {
    @Indexed(unique=true)
    private String player_name;

    @RelatedTo(direction = Direction.BOTH, elementClass = Player.
class)
    private Set<Player> coPlayers;

    public Player() {}
    public Player(String player_name) { this.player_name = player_
name; }

    private void playedWith(Player coPlayer) { coPlayers.
add(coPlayer); }
}

Player ronaldo = new Player("Ronaldo").persist();
Player beckham = new Player("Beckham").persist();
Player rooney = new Player("Rooney").persist();

beckham.playedWith(ronaldo);
beckham.playedWith(rooney);

// Persist creates relationships to graph database
beckham.persist();

for (Player coPlayer : beckham.getFriends()) {
    System.out.println("Friend: " + coPlayer);
}

// The Method findAllByTraversal() is part of @NodeEntity
for (Player coPlayer : ronaldo.findAllByTraversal(Player.class,
        Traversal.description().evaluator(Evaluators.
includingDepths(1, 2)))) {
    System.out.println("Ronaldo's coPlayers to depth 2: " + coPlayer);
}

// Add <datagraph:repositories base-package="com.your.repo"/> to
context config.
```

```
interface com.example.repo.PlayerRepository extends
GraphRepository<Player> {}

@Autowired PlayerRepository repo;
beckham = repo.findByPropertyValue("player_name", "beckham");
long numberOfPeople = repo.count();
```

The preceding code denotes a scenario where we relate players who have played together. The SDN domain class defines the Node entity along with its data and indexes and relationships. The `persist()` method creates the entities into the database. Apart from the basic CRUD operations, you can also run Cypher queries with SDN if you have included the REST library in your dependency list for the project:

```
@Query("start movie=node({self}) match
        movie-->genre<--similar return similar")
Iterable<Movie> similarMovies;
```

SDN is a highly efficient framework built on top of Spring; however, when you want to load larger datasets into such applications, you might find things getting a bit complex. In Neo4j, the batch inserter is the answer to bulk data loads, but SDN does not support batch inserter out of the box. SDN is simply a layer of mapping between the Neo4j entities and the Java types. You need to explicitly write code to insert data in batches using `TypeRepresentationStrategy` defined for the nodes and relationships, which creates a __type__ property for the defined entities and __type__ indexes for nodes and relationships. You can look further into these issues at `http://projects.spring.io/spring-data-Neo4j/`.

Summary

It's one thing to handle and store big data and a different one to understand it. This is where Neo4j comes in handy as a super tool. In this chapter, we saw that not only can you store your data in a more organized and logical manner, you can also easily interpret the relationships that exist in the data with minimal efforts. So, as the data grows in size, a graph database can make life easier for an analyst and a developer. We looked at techniques that need to be kept in mind while developing applications to handle large volumes of graph data.

In the next chapter, we will take a look at how you can go about testing the Neo4j applications that you have built or are about to build. You will also learn about the options available for scaling a Neo4j graph database.

5
Testing and Scaling Neo4j Applications

When graph databases came into the picture, testing was an unchartered territory and developers had a hard time ensuring that applications were configured in a failsafe manner. With the introduction of several highly efficient graph data stores, including Titan and Neo4j, several projects and frameworks sprung up in addition to the built-in ones. Neo4j in particular is ACID in nature, transaction-friendly and easy to set up, but a viable testing framework is always useful to ensure that your application runs as intended and helps to identify hidden bugs. In this chapter, we will cover the following topics related to the testing of Neo4j applications:

- Testing Neo4j applications with the GraphAware Framework
- Unit testing with the Java API and GraphUnit
- Performance testing
- Benchmarking performance with Gatling
- Scaling options for Neo4j applications

Testing Neo4j applications

Neo4j as a graph database has several powerful and reliable features. Although it does include a basic unit testing module for embedded applications, the support for testing has still not made it into the core packages yet. You might not feel the need to test your applications if they seem to work on your local machines. However, it is always wise to have a rigorous testing scheme when your application is deployed on a larger or production scale or is handling critical data and huge traffic loads. So, when the need for testing arose for Neo4j, **GraphAware** came up with an advanced framework built on top of the core Neo4j libraries, but also included several advanced optimizations and features. Among them was the GraphAware server that allowed developers to build **Representational State Transfer (REST)** API applications on top of the Spring MVC framework, in place of the earlier used JAX-RS. They also included a GraphAware runtime that provided customized modules for improved transactions and continuous graph computations on both embedded and server environments. In addition, it also provides a GraphAware testing framework that was available only for Java-based development before. So, embedded instances of Neo4j in applications, Spring-MVC-controlled applications, and extension development can be easily tested using this framework. The GraphAware framework speeds up application development with Neo4j by extending a platform to developers to create generic or domain-specific functionalities, analytical applications, advanced graph computation algorithms, and much more. The GraphAware test framework provides the flexibility to easily test code that interacts with the Neo4j database in any way. If you are a developer who is writing or planning to write Java code for Neo4j applications, or are developing modules for the GraphAware Framework and its APIs, then this testing framework is going to make your life easier. To include this testing module in your project, you can use **Maven** to specify it as a dependency in your pom.xml file:

```
<dependency>
    <groupId>com.graphaware.neo4j</groupId>
    <artifactId>tests</artifactId>
    <version>2.1.4.17</version>
    <scope>test</scope>
</dependency>
```

 Check for the latest version number of the GraphAware Framework from http://graphaware.com/downloads/ when including the Maven dependency in the pom.xml file.

You can now work with unit, performance, and integration testing for your Neo4j applications.

Unit testing

Unit testing works on the smallest testable parts of the code that deal with few inputs and a single output. When you modify Neo4j data stores using Java code, especially in embedded applications, you make use of the `ImpermanentGraphDatabase` file together with Neo4j APIs to test the code. The APIs you can use include the Java API, is the Neo4j traversal framework, and Cypher. The REST API does not much use with Java code. As an alternative, you can use GraphUnit to perform the integration testing. We will take a look at both scenarios in the following sections. For the purpose of testing, let's take an example graph that initially creates two nodes and a relationship to connect them and sets properties on the nodes and the relationship. The assertions that a unit test would apply on this graph and its functionality would be:

- The creation of nodes and relationships was as expected, and the properties and labels were set correctly

- No additional entities were created or set, including nodes, relationships, properties, and labels

- The already existing sections of the graph, if any, remain unaltered

Not all the preceding objectives can be fulfilled by the use of Cypher. This is because Cypher is created for declarative operations on the graph database and not for imperative ones. So, only the first criterion can be fulfilled. It is also important to note that asserting the existence of an entity in the database is simple, but the process of ensuring that no extra entities were created, or no extra labels and properties were set is a rather difficult task.

So, unit tests can be performed by asserting the graph state using the low-level native Java APIs. Let's see how we can test using the Java API and the GraphUnit framework.

Using the Java API

In order to use the testing facilities on an impermanent graph, the `tests.jar` file of the neo4j-kernel must be present on the classpath for use. It uses the standard JUnit fixtures to achieve the testing. This can be included in your project using the Maven dependency along with JUnit, as follows:

```
<dependency>
    <groupId>org.neo4j</groupId>
    <artifactId>neo4j-kernel</artifactId>
    <version>2.1.4</version>
    <scope>test</scope>
```

```
        <type>test-jar</type>
    </dependency>
```

 Note that the `<type>test-jar</type>` inclusion is important, without this you would include neo4j-kernel but not the testing libraries.

A new database can be created for testing purposes, which will be stopped after the tests are complete. Although, it is possible to use the database being tested upon for intermediate operations, it is not advised to do this since it can cause conflicts and unnecessary writes.

```
@Before
public void prepareTestDatabase(){
    graphDb = new TestGraphDatabaseFactory().newImpermanentDatabase();
}


@After
public void destroyTestDatabase(){
    graphDb.shutdown();
}
```

In the process of testing, you create nodes and assert their existence, while enclosing the write operations in a transaction:

```
Node n = null;
try ( Transaction tx = graphDb.beginTx() )
{
    n = graphDb.createNode();
    n.setProperty( "title", "Developer" );
    tx.success();
}

// Check for a valid node Id
assertThat( n.getId(), is( greaterThan( -1L ) ) );

// A node is retrieved with the Id of the node created. The id's and
// property must be matching.
try ( Transaction tx = graphDb.beginTx() )
{
    Node foundNode = graphDb.getNodeById( n.getId() );
    assertThat( foundNode.getId(), is( n.getId() ) );
    assertThat( (String) foundNode.getProperty( "title" ), is(
"Developer" ) );
}
```

GraphUnit-based unit testing

GraphUnit contains a set of assertion methods that are useful in creating Neo4j tests. What they basically do is compare whether the graph created is the same as the graph that should be created. GraphUnit addresses the unit testing problems, thus ensuring that no extra properties, nodes, or relationships were altered in the graph. It gives developers the opportunity to express the desired state of the graph using Cypher and assert that this is indeed the case. The following method is used for this purpose:

```
public static void assertSameGraph(GraphDatabaseService database,
String sameGraphCypher)
```

The first parameter is the **database** whose state is being asserted. The second parameter is a **Cypher** (typically CREATE) statement that expresses the desired state of the database. The graph in the database and the graph that should be created by the Cypher statement must be identical in order for the unit test to pass. Of course, the internal Neo4j node and relationship IDs are excluded from any comparisons.

If tests on graphs are large and if it is not the developer's intention to verify the state of the entire graph, GraphUnit provides another method:

```
public static void assertSubgraph(GraphDatabaseService database,
String subgraphCypher)
```

The idea is the same, except that there are additional relationships and nodes in the database that are not expressed in the Cypher statement. However, the Cypher-defined subgraph must be present in the database with exactly the same node labels, relationship types, and properties on both nodes and relationships in order for the test to pass.

 For more insights into the set of assertion methods, you can visit http://graphaware.com/site/framework/latest/apidocs/com/graphaware/test/unit/GraphUnit.html.

Unit testing an embedded database

We can perform a simple unit test to assert that a pairing has been successfully saved. A pairing is formed with two entities that represent nodes. Each entity has a name and a directed relation between the entities. This structure is illustrated in the following figure:

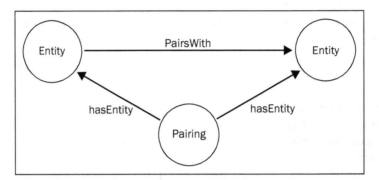

The code to test this simple structure using the Java API is large and is difficult to maintain for extended time periods. GraphUnit, on the other hand, enables you to compare the current graph state to the subgraph that you intended to create, which can be represented with the help of a Cypher statement. So, all you need to do is write a Cypher statement to create a subgraph that contains the two entities along with a pairing and use it as an argument to the `assertSameGraph()` method:

```
String entitySubgraph = "create (e1:Entity {name: 'Ferrari'}),
(e2:Entity {name: 'Aston Martin'}), " + "(e1)<-[:hasEntity]-(p:Pairing
{affinity: 0.50, allAffinities: [0.50]}), " + "(p)-[:hasEntity]->(e2)
merge (e1)-[:pairsWith]-(e2)";
GraphUnit.assertSameGraph(getGraphDb(), entitySubgraph);
```

This will ensure that the structure represented by the Cypher query string is all that constitutes the graph that was created, with every property matching exactly.

GraphUnit contains another method to check whether the Neo4j graph contains a desired subgraph in it. This will assert the existence of the subgraph specified by the cypher query and filter out the other nodes and relationships:

```
GraphUnit.assertSubgraph(getGraphDb(), entitySubgraph);
```

GraphUnit needs an `org.neo4j.graphdb.GraphDataService` handle to the database that needs to tested. It can be used effectively with the impermanent or embedded graph databases. To test server instances of Neo4j using the REST API, we can use GraphAware RestTest, which we will discuss later in the chapter.

Apart from basic code testing, GraphUnit can also be used to verify that the import of data into a graph completes successfully or not. Since data import from CSV or other formats is not performed as transactions, this is important to check the integrity of the data load process. So, you can use GraphUnit to write a single unit test that verifies the subgraphs in the database created after the import, rather than inspecting the graph visually or running queries to check.

```
public class graphUnitTestDemo
{
   @Test
   public void testActor()
     {
       String actorSubgraph = "Match (country:Country {name:
'BRITAIN'})<-[:From]-(actor {name: 'PIERCE BROSNAN'}), (m:Movie
{id: 5}), (min:Minutes {id: 35}) create (actor)-[:ActedIn]-
>(genre:Genre{type: 'Action'})-[:In]->(m) create (m)-[:BelongsTo]-
>(country)";
       GraphUnit.assertSubgraph(getGraphDb(), actorSubgraph);
     }
   @Test
   public void testReferee()
     {
       String refSubgraph = "Match (m:Movie {id:5}) match (c:Country
{name:'BRITAIN'}) create (m)-[:Director]->(d:Director {name:'The
Doctor'})-[:HomeCountry]->(c)";
       GraphUnit.assertSameGraph(getGraphDb(), refSubgraph);
     }
}
```

This is a much simpler, convenient, and effective way to test the graph at hand.

There are several benefits of this testing technique, especially concerning readability. Moreover, the GraphUnit version for testing is actually more fail-safe since it results in failure, when the graph contents are more than or different to that explicitly mentioned in the Cypher statement.

Unit testing a Neo4J server

The GraphAware RestTest library was created to test code that is designed to connect to a standalone server instance of Neo4j. You can set up the testing functionality on your Neo4j server by including the following JAR files in the plugins directory:

- `graphaware-resttest-2.1.3.15.6.jar`

- `graphaware-server-community-all-2.1.3.15.jar` (or `graphaware-server-enterprise-all-2.1.3.15.jar`, depending upon your server installation.)

> You can download the JAR files from `http://graphaware.com/downloads/`. Check the latest versions of the JAR files while downloading. You will also need to restart your server after dropping the preceding JAR files in the plugins directory to be able to use the APIs.

The testing process is pretty simple. You can direct POST requests to the predefined URLs defined in the RestTest framework to check a specific functionality. In the server mode deployment, there are three URLs defined that you can use:

- `http://server-ip-address:7474/graphaware/resttest/clear` in order to clear the database.

- `http://server-ip-address:7474/graphaware/resttest/assertSameGraph` in order to assert the database state. The body of the request must contain a URL-encoded Cypher CREATE statement defining the expected state of the graph.

- `http://server-ip-address:7474/graphaware/resttest/assertSubgraph` in order to assert the database state for a given subgraph. The body of the request must contain a URL-encoded Cypher CREATE statement to define the state of the subgraph.

A call to the first API endpoint will clear the database. The second API endpoint provides a functionality that is similar to the `assertSameGraph()` method of GraphUnit. This helps verify that the graph existing in the database matches the one that will be created through the Cypher CREATE statement included in the request body. Every aspect of the graph, including nodes, relationships, their labels and properties, needs to be exactly the same. However, the internal IDs that Neo4j uses to reference nodes/relationships are ignored while matching the graphs. If the matching is successful, the response returned is an OK(200) HTTP response. Otherwise, if the assertion fails, an **EXPECTATION_FAILED** HTTP response is returned with a status code of 417.

In the third endpoint case, the RestTest API validates whether the graph structure created by the Cypher query provided is a subgraph of the graph in the database server. This is equivalent to the `assertSubGraph()` method of the GraphUnit API. The response code of the outcomes are the same as mentioned previously.

Performance testing

Apart from the validity and correctness of your code units, it is also essential at times to run database jobs to analyze how queries, operations, and the database itself is performing. These include mission critical operations such as banking, financial analytics, and real-time datasets, where errors can be catastrophic. This is, however, not a simple task. A database is a complex ecosystem that incorporates many moving entities, namely transaction sizes, frequency of commits, database content, type, and size of cache. The GraphAware Testing framework also provides the `PerformanceTestSuite` and `PerformanceTest` classes to make the performance testing process simple.

To deal with moving entities, the tests can define a parameter list that contains the desired entity. The test framework will then proceed to generate every possible permutation and use each of them to run the performance test a number of times. Among other things, in the performance tests you implement, you can specify the following entities as parameters:

- The number of times to run the tests and get performance metrics
- The number of dry runs to perform so that a warm cache is established to test speed of cache retrievals
- The parameters that are to be used
- When to discard the test database and build a new one

Here's a simple example of performance test code that you can write:

```
public class PerformanceTestDemo implements PerformanceTest {
    enum Scenario {
        FIRST_SCENARIO,
        OTHER_SCENARIO
    }
     /**{@inheritDoc}*/
    @Override
    public String longName() {return "Test Long Name";}
    /**{@inheritDoc}*/
    @Override
    public String shortName() {return "test-short-name";}
```

```java
    /**{@inheritDoc}*/
    @Override
    public List<Parameter> parameters() {
        List<Parameter> result = new LinkedList<>();
        result.add(new CacheParameter("cache")); //no cache, low-level
cache, high-level cache
        result.add(new EnumParameter("scenario", Scenario.class));
        return result;
    }


    /**{@inheritDoc}*/
    @Override
    public int dryRuns(Map<String, Object> params) {
        return ((CacheConfiguration) params.get("cache")).
needsWarmup() ? 10000 : 100;
    }
    /**{@inheritDoc}*/
    @Override
    public int measuredRuns() {
        return 100;
    }
    /**{@inheritDoc}*/
    @Override
    public Map<String, String> databaseParameters(Map<String, Object>
params) {
        return ((CacheConfiguration) params.get("cache")).addToConfig(
Collections.<String, String>emptyMap());
    }
    /**{@inheritDoc}*/
    @Override
    public void prepareDatabase(GraphDatabaseService database, final
Map<String, Object> params) {
        //create 100 nodes in batches of 100
        new NoInputBatchTransactionExecutor(database, 100, 100, new
UnitOfWork<NullItem>() {
            @Override
            public void execute(GraphDatabaseService database,
NullItem input, int batchNumber, int stepNumber) {
                database.createNode();
            }
        }).execute();
    }
    /**{@inheritDoc}*/
    @Override
```

```
    public RebuildDatabase rebuildDatabase() {
        return RebuildDatabase.AFTER_PARAM_CHANGE;
    }
    /**{@inheritDoc}*/
    @Override
    public long run(GraphDatabaseService database, Map<String, Object>
params) {
        Scenario scenario = (Scenario) params.get("scenario");
        switch (scenario) {
            case FIRST_SCENARIO:
                //run test for scenario 1
                return 20; //the time it takes in microseconds
            case OTHER_SCENARIO:
                //run test for scenario 2
                return 20; //the time it takes in microseconds
            default:
                throw new IllegalStateException("Unknown scenario");
        }
    }
    /**{@inheritDoc}*/
    @Override
    public boolean rebuildDatabase(Map<String, Object> params) {
        throw new UnsupportedOperationException("never needed,
database rebuilt after every param change");
    }
}
```

You change the run method implementation to do some real work. Then add this test to a test suite and run it:

```
public class RunningDemoTest extends PerformanceTestSuite {
    /**{@inheritDoc}*/
    @Override
    protected PerformanceTest[] getPerfTests() {
        return new PerformanceTest[]{new PerformanceTestDemo()};
    }
}
```

This example code skeleton shows a custom class that implements the `PerformanceTest` class of the GraphAware library, which overrides the methods that need to be tweaked according to your requirement. The result is a total of 6 parameter permutations (the product of 2 scenarios and 3 cache types), each executed 100 times, as we have defined. When the test run process is complete, a file with the name `test-short-name-***.txt` (*** being the timestamp) appears in the project root directory. The file contains the runtimes of each test round for the parameter permutations. For example, the `Test Long Name` result file would contain something like this:

```
cache;scenario;times in microseconds...
nocache;FIRST_SCENARIO;15;15;15;15;15;15;15;...
nocache;OTHER_SCENARIO;15;15;15;15;15;15;15;...
lowcache;FIRST_SCENARIO;15;15;15;15;15;15;15;...
lowcache;OTHER_SCENARIO;15;15;15;15;15;15;15;...
highcache;FIRST_SCENARIO;15;15;15;15;15;15;15;...
highcache;OTHER_SCENARIO;15;15;15;15;15;15;15;...
```

It is also worth noting that Facebook has open sourced a benchmarking tool for social graph databases called **LinkBench**, which makes it possible for the Neo4j community to compare their performance metrics with a real and large dataset. You can check out the details of this system at `https://github.com/graphaware/linkbench-neo4j`.

Benchmarking performance with Gatling

With Benchmarking, we can compare our Neo4j process and performance metrics with stats from other players in the industry. It is a method to measure the quality, time, and cost of implementing a solution in a production scenario. It is also a useful measure to constantly evaluate your needs and the current system metrics to analyze when a change might be required to hardware or software tools.

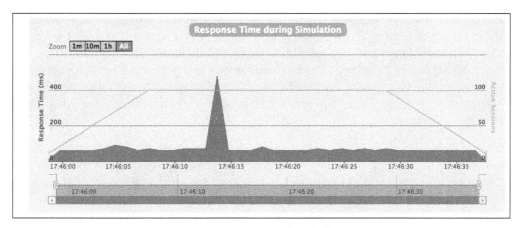

Response time metrics from Gatling

Although the Neo4j dashboard gives a good idea of the database state and metrics, you can use Gatling, a load testing framework based on Scala, Netty, and Akka that can test your whole application to measure end-to-end performance. The only challenge of this tool is that you need to write your code in Scala. You can use the built-in HTTP library to send requests to the REST server and evaluate the response and create simulations in real time to measure performance. You can learn about Gatling in detail at `http://gatling.io/`. Gatling also provides a splendid interface to view your metrics graphically; the following are some examples:

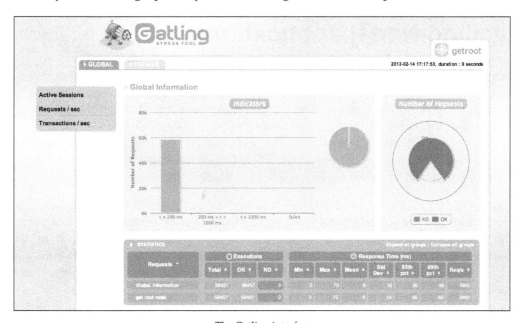

The Gatling interface

What we take away from the entire performance testing and benchmarking processes is the prospect of finding loopholes and bottlenecks in the system. We can then apply tweaks and tools to get the Neo4j system run more efficiently. Like any complex system, Neo4j can be properly tuned to achieve optimal performance. When you view the time-varying performance of your graph data store based on the workload characteristics, you can figure out whether it is possible to amortize your setup steps across many queries.

There are several tweaks possible that can help in increasing the performance of the Neo4j system depending on the type of data stored, the size of data, or the type of query operations performed on the data. However, here are a couple of common generic techniques that can help improve the performance of the Neo4j subsystem:

- **Warm cache**: This refers to creating a cache of the relevant and most updated data in the database, thereby reducing the lookup time for most parts of the requests. Benchmarking should measure the empty and warm caching behavior of your Neo4j system to provide an good performance metric.

- **Simpler algorithms**: Sometimes, blips in performance metrics are not always the fault of the database or data, but that of the application-specific algorithms you use. It is obvious that the algorithms that fit your database must be chosen, but complexity and sophistication define performance too. Think of graph traversals!

Scaling Neo4j applications

Large datasets in the Neo4j world refer to those that are substantially larger compared to the main memory of the system. In scenarios with such datasets, it is not possible for the Neo4j system to cache the entire database in memory, thereby providing blazingly fast traversals on the graph, because it will eventually lead to disk operations. Earlier, it was recommended to scale the system vertically using more RAM or solid state drives that have much lower seek times for the data on the disk compared to spinning drives. While SSDs considerably increase performance, even the fastest SSDs cannot replace the RAM, which in the end is the limiting factor.

In order to service huge workloads and manage large sets of data in Neo4j, partitioning graphs across multiple physical instances seem complex way to scale graph data. In versions up to 1.2, scaling seemed to be the con of this graph data store, but with the introduction of Neo4j **High Availability (HA)**, there has been significant insight to handling large datasets and design solutions for scalability and availability.

One significant pattern that uses Neo4j HA is **cache sharding**, which is used to maintain increased performance with massive datasets that exceed the available main memory space of the system. Cache sharding is not the traditional sharding that most databases implement today. This is due to the fact that it expects a complete dataset to be present on each instance of the database. Instead, to implement cache sharding, the workload is partitioned among each database instance in order to increase the chances of hitting a warm cache for a particular request; believe it or not, warm caches in Neo4j give extremely high performance.

There are several issues that Neo4j HA addresses, the following being the prominent features:

- It implements a *fault-tolerant* architecture for the database, in which you can configure multiple Neo4j slave database instances to be exact replica sets of a single Neo4j master database. Hence, the end user application that runs Neo4j will be perfectly operational when there is a hardware failure.

- It provides a read-mostly, horizontally scaling architecture that facilitates the system to handle much higher read traffic as compared to a single instance of the Neo4j database, since every instance contains a complete graph dataset.

In other words, cache sharding refers to the injection of some logic into the load balancer of the high availability cluster of Neo4j, thereby directing queries to some specific node in the cluster based on a rule or property (such as sessions or start values). If implemented properly, each node in the cluster will be able to house a part of the total graph in the corresponding object cache so that the required traversal can be made.

The architecture for this solution is represented in the following figure. Thus, instead of typical graph sharding, we reduce the solution to that of consistent routing, which is a technique that has been in use with web farms for ages.

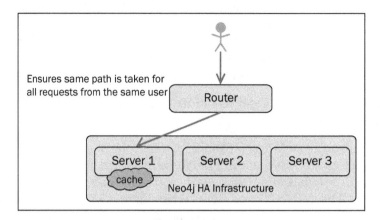

The logic that is used to perform the routing varies according to the domain of the data. At times, you can use specific characteristics of the data, such as label names or indexes for routing, whereas sometimes, sticky sessions are good enough. One simple technique is the database instance that serves a request for the first time for some user will also serve all subsequent requests for that user, with a high probability of processing the requests from a warm cache. You can use domain knowledge of the requests to route, for example, in the case of geographical or location-specific data, you route requests that pertain to particular locations to Neo4j instances that have data for that location in their warm cache. In a way, we are shooting up the likelihood of nodes and relationships being cached and hence, it becomes faster to access and process.

Apart from reading from the databases, to run multiple servers to harness the caching capabilities, we also need to sync data between these servers. This is where Neo4j HA comes into play. Effectively, with the deployment of Neo4J HA, a multimaster cluster is formed. A write to any instance propagates the write with the help of the HA protocol. When the elected master in the cluster is being written to, the data is first persisted there due to its ACID nature, and then, the modification is eventually transferred to the slaves through the HA protocol in order to maintain consistency.

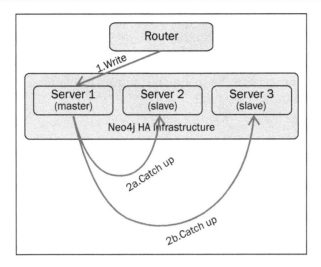

If a cluster slave mode processes a write operation, then it updates the elected master node with the help of a transaction, and initially, the results are persisted in both. Other slaves are updated from the master with the use of the HA protocol.

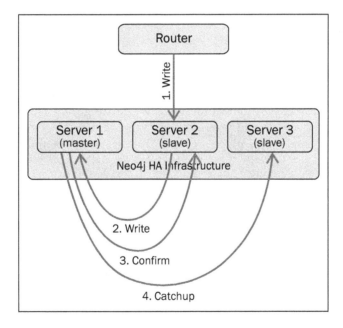

With the use of such a pattern, a Neo4J HA cluster acts as a high-performance database for efficient read-write operations. Additionally, a good strategy for routing, it helps to perform in-memory and blazingly fast traversals for applications.

The following is a summary of the scaling techniques implemented, depending on the data at hand and the cost strategy:

Type 1:

Dataset size: Order of tens of GBs

Strategy: Scale a single machine vertically with more RAM

Reason: Most server racks contain the RAM of the order of 128 GB for a typical machine. Since Neo4j loves RAM for data caching, where O (dataset) ≈ O (memory), all of the data can be cached into memory, and operations on it can take place at extremely high speeds.

Weaknesses: Clustering needed for availability; disk performance limits the write scalability

Type 2:

Dataset size: Order of hundreds of GBs

Strategy: Cache sharding techniques

Reasoning: The data is too big to fit in the RAM of a single machine, but is possible to replicate onto disks of many machines. Cache sharding increases the chances of hitting a warm cache in order to provide high performance. Cache misses, however, are not critical and can be optimized using SSDs in the place of spinning disks.

Weaknesses: You need a router/load balancer in the Neo4j infrastructure for consistent routing.

Type 3:

Dataset size: TBs and more

Strategy: Sharding based on domain-specific knowledge

Reasoning: With such large datasets, which are not replicable across instances, sharding provides a way out. However, since there is no algorithm (yet) to arbitrarily shard graph data, we depend on the knowledge of the domain in order to predict which node to allocate to which machine or instance.

Weaknesses: It is difficult to classify or relate all domains for sharding purposes.

In most scenarios that developers face, these heuristics are a good choice. It's simple to calculate the scale of your data and accordingly plan a suitable Neo4j deployment. It also provides a glimpse into the future of connected data—while most enterprises dealing with connected data are in the tens to hundreds of GB segments, with the current rate, there will soon be a requirement for greater data-crunching techniques.

Summary

In this chapter, you learned that testing, though it might seem unimportant, is essential and rather simple for graph data in Neo4j applications. You also learned about the Neo4j framework from GraphAware including the GraphUnit testing libraries for Unit tests. We saw how to test the performance of the Neo4j system and an introduction to benchmarking it using Gatling to obtain performance metrics. We also looked at ways to scale Neo4j applications, with Cache Sharding being an essential technique.

In the next chapter, we will be digging into the internals of Neo4j which affect the processing, storage, APIs, and performance of this amazing graph database.

6
Neo4j Internals

Databases are constantly growing around real-world storage techniques and believed to be one of the complex accomplishments of engineering. Graph databases such as Neo4j are taking connected data storage to an entirely different level. However, most of us who work with Neo4j are left wondering about how it all works internally, because there is practically no documentation about the internal architecture of components. The kernel code base is not enormous and can be analyzed, but it is always good to have a guide to provide us with an understanding of the classes while abstracting the implementation details. Now that we have seen how we can use Neo4j as an efficient and secure data store for connected data, let's take a look at what lies under the hood and what goes on when you store, query, or traverse a graph data store. The way Neo4j stores data in the form of nodes and relationships inherently is intriguing and efficient, and you will get a great working knowledge of it if you try reading through the source. In this chapter, touching upon the core functionality, we will cover the following topics about the internal structure and working of the Neo4j database:

- The property store structure
- How caching works
- Memory and the API functionality
- Transaction and its components
- High availability and election of HA master

Introduction to Neo4j internals

It might look an efficient and beautiful solution for end users and developers, but, internally, it is a completely different story. The way the modules and submodules are interconnected is an interesting study. If you have a knack for tinkering with code and an understanding of Java, then you can yourself analyze the classes in the source code of Neo4j, which can be found at `https://github.com/neo4j/neo4j`.

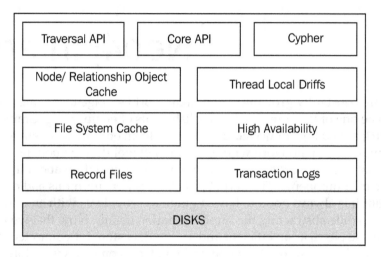

Working of your code

Let's take a look at a simple **Hello World** application code for Neo4j and understand what goes on under the hood when you try to perform some simple operations on Neo4j through the Java API. Here is the code for a sample app:

```
import org.neo4j.graphdb.*;
import org.neo4j.kernel.EmbeddedGraphDatabase;

/**
 * Example class that constructs a simple graph with
 * message attributes and then prints them.
```

```
*/

public class NeoOneMinute {
  public enum MyRelationshipTypes implements RelationshipType {
    KNOWS
  }

  public static void main(String[] args) {
    GraphDatabaseService graphDb = new EmbeddedGraphDatabase("var/
base");
    Transaction tx = graphDb.beginTx();
    try {
      Node node1 = graphDb.createNode();
      Node node2 = graphDb.createNode();
      Relationship someRel = node1.createRelationshipTo(node2,
MyRelationshipTypes.KNOWS);

      node1.setProperty("message", "Hello, ");
      node2.setProperty("message", "world!");
      someRel.setProperty("message", "brave Neo4j ");
      tx.success();

      System.out.print(node1.getProperty("message"));
      System.out.print(someRel.getProperty("message"));
      System.out.print(node2.getProperty("message"));
      }
    finally {
      tx.finish();
      graphDb.shutdown();
      }
    }
  }
```

The initiating point in the Neo4j program is the database service object
defined from `org.neo4j.graphdb.GraphDatabaseService` and referred to as
`GraphDatabaseService`. All the core functionalities for nodes, IDs, transactions and
so on are exposed through this interface. This object is a wrapper over a few other
classes and interfaces, `GraphDbInstance` being one of them, which starts with the
config map that the user provides (empty in the preceding case). The `org.neo4j.`
`kernel.AutoConfigurator` object then receives this, and the memory to be used
for memory-mapped buffers is computed from JVM statistics. You can change this
behavior by setting a `false` value for the `use_memory_mapped_buffers` flag, causing
the config map to be passed to an object of the `org.neo4j.kernel.Config` class.

GraphDbModule, the TxModule for transactions, the manager objects for cache, persistence, and locking (CacheManager, PersistenceModule, LockManager, respectively) are then created and sustained until the application's execution ends. If no errors are thrown, then the embedded database has been initiated.

Node and relationship management

NodeManager (defined in the org.neo4j.kernel.impl.core.NodeManager class) is one of the most crucial and large classes in the Neo4j source that provides an abstraction for the caching and the underlying persistent storage-exposing methods to operate on nodes and relationships. The configuration that is passed is then parsed and the caching for the nodes and relationships is initialized by figuring out their sizes. AdaptiveCacheManager abstracts the sizing issue of the caches. NodeManager handles the locking operations with the help of lock stripping. In order to maintain a balance between the level of concurrency and the performance of memory, an array stores ReentrantLocks and, depending upon the integral ID values of the node or the relationship, locking is performed by hashing over it. When you invoke the getNodeById() or getRelationshipById() method, it roughly follows these steps:

1. The cache is checked. If the entity already exists in the cache, it is returned from there.

2. Based on the ID passed as a parameter, a lock is acquired.

3. The cache is checked again. If it has currently come into existence, then it is returned (since multithreaded operations occur!).

4. The manager class is requested for persistent storage for the required entity. If unavailable, NotFoundException is thrown.

5. The retrieved value is returned in the form of an appropriate implementation plan.

6. The retrieved value is cached.

7. The lock is then released and the value is returned to the calling method.

This is the gist of the main work of NodeManager. However it is intended to be used to perform many other operations that are beyond the scope of this book, but you can check them out in the source.

Implementation specifics

The Node and Relationship interfaces defined in org.neo4j.graphdb provide implementations for NodeProxy and RelationshipProxy and contain the unique IDs for the nodes or relationships that are represented by them. They are used in the propagation of the method calls of the interface to the NodeManager object that is being used. This integral ID is what is returned from the method calls that are executed every time a node, relationship, or property is added to EmbeddedGraphDatabase.

Nodes and relationships also use the NodeImpl and RelationshipImpl classes defined in the org.neo4j.kernel.impl.core package; this package extends the core Primitive class to provide abstract implementations of Properties and help to delegate the loading and storing of property values to the object of NodeManager. It holds the value of the ID and is extended by the implementation classes (NodeImpl and RelationshipImpl), each of which implements the abstract methods accordingly along with operation-specific functions (for example, the NodeImpl class has a getRelationships() method while the RelationshipImpl class has getStartNode()).

These are some of the types of implementations that NodeManager handles internally.

Storage for properties

The property storage of Neo4j has seen several upgrades and improvements with recent releases, which has made it more usable and stable, while optimizing the layer to use lesser disk space without compromising on features, and improving the speed of operations.

The storage structure

Originally, the Neo4j property store was in the form of a doubly linked list, in which the nodes contained additional information about the structure, along with the property-related data. The node structure then is represented in the following format:

Byte(s)	Information
0	The 4 high bits of the previous pointer and inUse flag
1	unused
2	The 4 high bits of next pointer
3-4	The type of property

Byte(s)	Information
5-8	The index of property
9-12	32 low bits of the previous pointer
13-16	32 low bits of the next pointer
17-24	Data for the property

So, the 8 bytes at the end were used to store the value and were sufficient to hold all primitive types, small strings, or pointer references to the dynamic store where long strings or arrays are stored. This, however, has a redundancy, since the complete 8 bytes are only utilized when the data stored is long, double, or string and references are repeated for each property. This causes significant overhead. So, in the newer versions of Neo4j, this was optimized by designing `PropertyRecord`, which, instead of housing a single property, now emulates a container to incorporate a number of properties of variable lengths. You can get a clearer outline of the present structure here:

Byte(s)	Information
0	4 high bits of the previous pointer and 4 high bits of the next pointer
1-4	The previous property record
5–8	The next property record
9–40	Payload

As you can see, the `inUse` flag has been done away with and the space is optimized to include the payload more efficiently. There are 4 blocks of 8 bytes in the payload, each of which are used in a different manner depending upon the type of data stored in the property. The type and index of the property are necessary and always required and hence occupy the first 3 bytes of the blocks and 4 high bits of the 4th byte, respectively. The value of the property is dependent on the data type being stored. If you are using a primitive that can be accommodated in 4 bytes, then the 4th byte's lower 4 bits are skipped and the remainder of the 4 bytes are used to store the value. However, when you are storing arrays and nonshort strings using `DynamicStore`, you need 36 bits for the storage of the reference that uses the total lower 4 bits of the 4th byte and the remaining 4 bytes. These provisions for 4 properties are stored in the same `PropertyRecord`, thereby increasing the space efficiency of the storage. However, if doubles and longs are what you intend to store, then the remaining 36 bits are skipped over and the subsequent block is used to store the value. This causes unnecessary space wastage, but its occurrence is rare and overall more efficient than the original storage structure.

`LongerShortString` is a newly introduced type, which is an extension of the `ShortString` operating principle, in which a string is initially scanned to figure out whether it falls within an encoding. If it does, then the encoding is performed and a header is stored for it that contains the length of the string, the ID in the encoding table, and finally the original string. However, the UTF8 encoding scheme is used when the three and a half blocks of the property block are insufficient for storage and `DynamicStringStore` is used. In the case of an array, we first determine the smallest number of bits that can be used to store the values in it and, in the process, we drop the leading zeroes and maintain the same length for each element. For example, when given the array [5,4,3,2,1], each element does not take a separate set of 32 bits; rather, they are stored in 3 bits each. Similarly, only a single bit is used to store Boolean-valued array elements. In the case of dynamic arrays, a similar concept is used. So, such a data value is stored in the following format:

Number of Bits	Stored Information
4	Enumeration storing type of entity
6	The array length
6	Bits used for each item
The remaining 16	Data elements

There is one secret we are yet to explore: the `inUse` flag. It is, in fact, a marker to indicate whether a property exists and is in use or not. Each block is marked to distinguish whether it is in use and, since we are allowed to delete properties, a zero signifies that the current property is not in use or deleted. Moreover, the blocks are stored onto the disk in a defragmented manner. So, if some property from a set of properties is deleted, only the remaining two are written to disk, and the deleted property's 1th byte of the first block that is not used is marked as a zero, which indicates that it is actually not used. If you take some time to explore the source code of the Neo4j project, you will find these implementation details and strategies in `WriteTransaction`.

Migrating to the new storage

In a rare case, if you are dealing with an older version of Neo4j and considering an upgrade to the newer architecture, it cannot happen without the need to change, remove, or replace the existing data. You will need to recreate the existing database. This ensures that existing files are not overwritten, guarantees crash-resistance, and also backs up data. This process is relatively simple: read all nodes, relationships, and properties for them and then convert them to the new format before storing them. In the migration process, the size is significantly reduced as the deleted entities are omitted, which is noticeable if a lot of deletions have been performed on the database and it is not restarted often. The code and logic for migration is included in the source code of the Neo4j kernel in the `org.neo4j.kernel.impl.storemigration` package, which you can run both as part of a generic startup or in a standalone manner. You will be required to set `"allow_store_upgrade"="true"` in your config and then you can successfully execute the migration scripts.

Caching internals

Neo4j implements a caching mechanism that stores nodes and relationships as useful, internal objects for rapid in-memory access. It also makes extensive use of the `java.nio` package, where native I/O is utilized to use memory outside the Java heap for mapped memory. **Least Recently Used (LRU)** is one of the simplest and most popular algorithms for implementation and rapid operations for caching needs. The Java-specific implementation makes use of the `SoftReference` and `WeakReference` objects, which are treated in a special manner by the garbage collector for memory reclamation. This principle is utilized in caches that grow rapidly to fill the heap but, when the demand for memory arises for more important tasks, reclamation takes place. So, there are no hard upper limits to caching of objects, while simultaneously making memory available for other operations. Neo4j caches work on this principle by default.

Cache types

Neo4j maintains two separate caches for nodes and relationships that can be configured to have a variable upper bound in terms of size, which can be configured by the `max_node_cache_size` and `max_relationship_cache_size` options of the database. The implementations of caching techniques in Neo4j can be explored in the `org.neo4j.kernel.impl.cache` package. Neo4j provides four different types of caches built into the default package:

Cache type	Property
NoCache	This is degenerate and stores nothing
LruCache	This utilizes LinkedHashMap of the java.util package along with a custom method to remove the oldest entry when deallocating space—removeEldestEntry(); this makes it an adaptable LRU cache
SoftLruCache	An LruCache using soft values to store references and queues for garbage-collected reference instances
WeakLruCache	An LruCache using hard values to store references and queues for garbage-collected reference instances

Weak and soft references are the basis of the behavior of Java **Garbage Collector (GC)** depending on the references of an object. If the GC finds that an object is softly reachable, it might clear these references in an atomic manner to free up memory. However, if the GC finds an object to be weakly reachable, then it will clear all the weak references automatically and atomically.

The soft and weak LruCaches extend org.neo4j.kernel.impl.cache.ReferenceCache, including a pollClearedValues() method to get rid of dead references from the hashmap. If you need to explore the code, the cache contents are managed by the NodeManager class, while AdaptiveCacheManager handles memory consumptions and is configurable.

AdaptiveCacheManager

AdaptiveCacheManager manages the cache sets and their configurations along with adapting them to the size changes. A worker thread is spawned which, on every adaptive_cache_worker_sleep_time milliseconds (which is 3000 by default), wakes to re-adjust the size of the caches. In the case of ReferenceCaches, a call to the pollClearedValues() method is initiated. In the case of LruCache, the adaptSize() method is invoked on every cache and the size is re-adjusted depending upon the JVM memory statistics passed to the resize() method that removes elements until the new size is achieved.

The caching mechanism in Neo4j is mainly used to cache nodes and relationships implementations so that they can be retrieved from persistent storage and are completely abstracted by NodeManager.

Transactions

Transactions are an integral part of the Neo4j ecosystem and primarily dominated by the use of two major components — the **Write-Ahead Log (WAL)** and the **Wait-For Graph (WFG)** for detection of deadlocks prior to their occurrence.

The Write Ahead log

The WAL in the Neo4j transaction system ensures atomicity and durability in transactions. Every change during a transaction persists on disk as and when the request for the change is received, without modifying the database content. When the transaction is committed, the changes are made to the data store and subsequently removed from the disk. So, when the system fails during a commit, the transactions can be read back and database changes can be ensured. This guarantees atomic changes and durability of commit operations.

All the changes during transactions occur in *states*. On initiating a transaction (with the beginTx() method), a state called TX_STARTED is assigned to it. There are similar states assigned while preparing a transaction, committing it, and rolling it back. The changes stored during transactions are called commands. Every operation performed on the database including creation and deletion corresponds to a command and, collectively, they define what transactions are. In Neo4j, the WAL is implemented with the help of XaLogicalLog defined in org.neo4j.kernel.impl.transaction.xaframework in the source, which aids in the management of intermediate files for storage of commands during a transaction. The LogEntry class provides an abstraction over the way in which XaLogicalLog stores its information, which contains information for phases and stored commands of a transaction. So, whenever the transaction manager (txManager) indicates the change of a phase in a given transaction, or the addition of a command, it flags XaLogicalLog, which writes an appropriate entry to the file.

Basically, files are used to store transaction logs in the root directory of the database. The first file, nioneo_logical.log.active, is simply a marker that indicates which of the log files is currently active. The remaining are the active log files that follow the naming convention nioneo_logical.log.1 or nioneo_logical.log.2; only one of them is active at a given time and read and written to with the help of a memory buffer or heap as defined in the use_memory_mapped_buffers configuration parameter. Neo4j also has an option to maintain backup files in a versioned manner through the configuration parameter keep_logical_logs. They use the nioneo_logical.log.v<version_no> format to store the file. What logically happens is if you are set to store backups, your log files are not deleted after the transaction; instead, they are renamed to a backup file.

The logical log entries have an integral identifier for the transaction, assigned to them by XaLogicalLog. It also maintains xidIdentMap, which maps the identifier to the LogEntry.Start state in order to reference active transactions. Now it is evident that write operations are appended to the log after the file offset of the start entry. You can obtain all information about the transaction after the offset. So we can optimize the lookup time and store the offset of the Start entry along with xidIdentMap corresponding to the identifier for that transaction; we no longer need to scan the log file for the offset of the transaction and directly go to the indicated start of transaction. The LogEntry.Prepare state is achieved when the current transaction is being prepped for a commit. When the process of a transactional commit has been initiated, the state written can be LogEntry.OnePhaseCommit or LogEntry.TwoPhaseCommit, depending on whether we are writing to EmbeddedGraphDatabase or a distributed scenario (generally using a JTA/JTS service), respectively. When a transaction is completed and is no longer needed to exist in an active state, the LogEntry.Done state is written. At this state, the identifier to the start state is also removed from the map (xidIdentMap) where it was stored. LogEntry.Command is not a state as such, but a method for encapsulation of the transaction commands. The writeCommand() of XaLogicalLog takes in a command as an argument and writes it to disk.

The LogEntry state	Operation for trigger
Start	This indicates that the transaction is now active
Prepare	This indicates that the transaction is being prepped for a commit
OnePhaseCommit	This initiates a commit in EmbeddedGraphDatabase
TwoPhaseCommit	This initiates commits in a distributed scenario
Done	This indicates that a transaction is complete
Command (not an actual state)	Encapsulation for the commands in the transaction

So, all the state changes of a transaction are stored in the form of LogEntry that contains the state indicator flags and transaction identifier. No deletions occur whatsoever. Writing a **Done** state indicates that the transaction has passed. Also, the commands causing the state change are also persisted to disk.

We mentioned that all commands are appended with no deletions and the storage to disk can create massive files for large transactions. Well, that's where the concept of log rotation comes in, which is triggered once the size of the log file exceeds a threshold (the default value is 10 MB). The `rotate()` method of `XaLogicalLog` is invoked when the log file size exceeds the threshold during the appending of a command and there is no live transaction taking up any space greater than 5 MB. The `rotate()` function performs the following:

1. Checks the currently used log file from the .active file, which stores the reference.

2. Writes the content of the buffer for the log file to disk and creates the new log file with the version and identifier of the last committed transaction in the header.

3. Initiates reading of entries from the offset of Start. All `LogEntries` that belong to the current transaction are copied to the new log file and offset is updated accordingly.

4. Disposes of the previous log file and updates the reference to the new log file in the .active file.

All the operations are synchronized, which pauses all updating transactions till the rotate operations are over.

How does all this facilitate recovery? When termination of `XaLogicalLog` occurs, if the map is empty and no transactions are live, the `.active` file stores a marker that indicates the closure of the transaction, and the log files are removed. So, when a restart occurs, and the `.active` file is in the "nonclean" (or not closed) mode, it means that there are transactions pending. In this case, the last active log file is found from the `.active` file and the `doInternalRecovery()` method of `XaLogicalLog` is started. The dangling transactions are recreated and the transaction is reattempted.

The `setRecovered()` method is used to indicate that a transaction has been successfully recovered, which avoids its re-entry into the WAL during subsequent recovery processes.

Detecting deadlocks

Neo4j, being an ACID database solution, needs to ensure that a transaction is completed (whether successfully or unsuccessfully), thereby stopping all active threads and avoiding deadlocks in the process. The core components that provide this functionality include `RWLock` (Read Write Lock), `LockManager`, and `RagManager` (Resource Allocation Graph Manager).

RWLock

RWLock provides an implementation of the Java ReentrantReadWriteLock for Neo4j, which allows concurrency in reading but single-threaded, exclusive write access to the locked resource. Being re-entrant in nature, it facilitates the holder of the lock to re-acquire the lock again. The lock also uses RagManager to detect whether waiting on a resource can lead to possible future deadlocks. Essentially, RWLock maintains a reference to the locking resources, that is, the threads and counts for read and write locks. If a request for the read lock is processed by some thread, it checks whether writes locks exist; if they do, then they should be held by the calling resource itself which, when true, make sure the lock is granted. Otherwise, RagManager is used to detect whether the thread can be allowed to wait without a deadlock scenario. Write locks are handled in a similar fashion. To release locks, the counts are reduced and waiting threads are invoked in a FIFO manner.

RAGManager

RAGManager operates with primarily the checkWaitOn() and checkWaitOnRecursive() utility methods. It is informed of all acquired and released locks on resources. Before invoking wait() on a thread, RWLock gets possible deadlock information from RAGManager. It is essentially a WFG that stores a graph of the resources and threads waiting on them. The checkWaitOn() method traverses the WFG to find whether a back edge exists to the candidate that needs a lock, in which case, a DeadlockDetectedException exception is raised, which terminates the thread. This leads to an assertion that the transaction will not complete, thereby enforcing atomicity. So, loops are avoided in a transaction.

LockManager

The sole purpose and existence of the LockManager class is the synchronization of RWLock accesses, or creation of the locks and, whenever required, passing an instance of the RAGManager and appropriate removal at times. At a high level of abstraction, Neo4j uses this class for the purpose of locking.

The scheme of locks and detection of deadlock simply ensures that the graph primitives are not granted locks in an order that can lead to a deadlock. It, however, does not protect you from the application-code-level deadlocks arising when you write multithreaded applications.

The `XaTransaction` class in Neo4j that is the central authority in the transactional behavior is `XaTransaction`. For any transaction that deals with a Neo4j resource, the fundamental structure is defined by this class, which deals with the holding of `XaLogicalLog` to persist the state of the transaction, its operations, and storage of the transaction identifier. It also includes the `addCommand()` method, which is used for normal transactional operations, and the `injectCommand()` method, which is used at the time of recovery. The core class in Neo4j, which implements `WriteTransaction` transactions extends the `XaTransaction` class, thereby exposing the extended interface. Two types of fields are dealt with here:

- **Records**: This stores an integer to record a map for a particular primitive, where the integer is the ID of the primitive
- **Commands**: These are stored in the form of command object lists

In the course of normal operations, the actions performed on a Neo4j primitive are stored in the form of record objects in the store. As per the operation, the record is modified and placed in its appropriate map. In the prepare stage, the records are transformed into commands and are put in the corresponding Command Object list. At this point, an apt `LogEntry.Command` state is written to `XaLogicalLog`. When `doCommit()` is invoked, the commands are executed individually, which releases the locks held and finally the commands are cleared. If a request for `doRollback()` is received, the records in the map are checked. If it has been flagged as created, the record's ID is freed by the underlying store and, subsequently, the command and record collections are cleared. So, if a transaction results in failure, an implicit rollback is initiated and `injectCommand()` is used to directly add the commands in the commands list prior to the next commit operation. The IDs that are not yet freed are recovered from `IdGenerator` of the underlying storage as and when the database is restarted.

Commands

The command class extends `XaCommand` to be used in `NeoStore`. The command class defines a way for storage in `LogBuffer`, reading back from it followed by execution. `NodeCommand` is treated differently from `RelationshipCommand` and likewise for every primitive. From the operations perspective, `NodeCommand` in command has two essential components to work with: `NodeRecord`, which stores the changes that need to be performed on the store and `NodeStore`, which persists the changes. When execution is initiated, the store is asked to perform updates on `NodeRecord`. To persist the command to disk, the `writeToFile()` method is used, which sets a marker to the entry and writes the record fields. In order to read it back, the `readCommand()` method is invoked, which restructures `NodeCommand`. Other primitive command types follow the same procedure of operation:

- `TransactionImpl`
- `TxManager`
- `TxLog`

We have seen that transactions can be implemented over `NeoStore`. Likewise, there can also be transactions over a Lucene Index. All these transactions can be committed. However, since the transactions between indexes and primitives are connected, if `WriteTransaction` results in failure, then `LuceneTransaction` must also fail and vice versa. The `TransactionalImpl` class takes care of this. Resources are added to `TransactionImpl` with the help of `enlistResource()`, which are bound together with the help of the **TwoPhaseCommit (2PC)** protocol and, when a commit operation is requested, all the enlisted resources are asked to get prepared and they return a status of whether the changes succeeded or not. When all return an OK, they proceed with the commit; otherwise, a rollback is initiated. Also, each time a transaction status change occurs, a notification is sent to `TxManager` and the corresponding record is added to `txLog`. This WAL is used for failure recovery. The identifier for `TransactionImpl` is called `globalId` and every resource that enlists with it is assigned a corresponding `branchId`, which are bound together as an abstraction called `Xid`. So, when a resource is enlisted for the first time, it calls `TxManager` and writes a record to `txLog` that marks the initiation of a new transaction. In the case of a failure, when a transaction needs to be reconstructed from the log, we can associate the transaction with the resources that were being managed by it.

`TxManager` abstracts the `TransactionalImpl` object from the program. On starting a new transaction, a `TransactionalImpl` object is created and mapped to the thread currently in execution. All methods in `TxManager` (except the resume method) automatically receive the `TransactionImpl` object. `TxLog` works in a similar fashion as `XaLogicalLog` with regard to the writing of entries and the rotation of files.

So, if your system crashes during the execution phase of commands in a transaction, without a rollback, then what happens? In such a situation, the complete transaction is replayed and the commands that were already executed before the failure would be processed again.

High availability

Neo4j in recent years has adapted to handling larger data in a more reliable manner with the introduction of the high availability mode. Its architecture and operations revolve around a core concept: the algorithm for master election. In this section, we will take a look at why we need the master and the algorithm based on which the master is elected.

HA and the need for a master

High availability in Neo4j replicates the graph on all the machines in the cluster and manages write operations between them. High availability does not decentralize the stored graph (which is called sharding); it replicates the complete graph. One machine in the replica set has the authority to receive and propagate updates as well as keep track of locks and context in transactions. This machine is referred to as the master in the HA cluster and the supreme entity that handles, monitors, and takes care of the resources in replica machines.

When you set up a Neo4j cluster, you do not need to designate a master or allocate specialized resources to particular machines. This would create a single point of failures and defeat the purpose of HA when the master fails. Rather, the cluster elects its own master node when needed in a dynamic manner.

The nodes in the cluster need to communicate and they make use of a method called atomic broadcasting, which is used to send messages to all instances in a reliable manner. It is reliable since there is no loss of messages, the ordering of the messages is preserved, and no messages are corrupt or duplicated. In a narrower perspective, the operations are handled by a service called `neo4j-coordinator`, which basically has the following objectives to take care of:

- A method to indicate that each machine in the cluster participates in HA, something like a heartbeat. Failure to send this indication indicates that the instance is unable to handle operations for the clusters.

- In Neo4j, the preceding method also helps to identify how many and which machines currently exist in the cluster.

- A notification system for use in broadcasting of alerts to the remaining cluster.

The master election

The master keeps the knowledge of the real graph, or the graph's most updated database version. The latest version is determined by the latest transaction ID that was executed. The ID for transactions can be a monotonically increasing entity, as they are serialized in nature, which causes the last committed transaction ID to reflect the database version. This information, however, is internally generated in the database, but we require some external priority-enforcing information to be used for elections in cases where two machines have the same transaction IDs for the latest one. The external information can vary from machine to machine, ranging from the machine's IP to its CPU ID presented in the form of a configurable parameter in Neo4j called `ha.server_id`. The Lower the value of the server ID of an instance, the higher will be its priority for being elected as master.

So, depending upon the irregular "heartbeat" received from the current master in the cluster, an instance can initiate an election and collect the last transaction ID from each cluster machine. The one having the largest value is the elected master, with the server ID acting as the tiebreaker. On election, the result is notified to the cluster and all the machines along with the new master execute the same algorithm. When the conclusion from all machines coincide, the notification is stopped.

Finally, let's see how atomic broadcast is implemented. Apache Zookeeper is used to implement the Atomic Broadcast protocol (around Version 1.8) that guarantees delivery of messages in an order. Zookeeper is capable of setting a watch on a file in its distributed hierarchical filesystem with provisions for notifications in the event of addition or deletion of nodes. However, later versions might be equipped with Neo4j's own atomic broadcast. In Neo4j, the first machine creates a node defined as the root of the cluster. An ephemeral node (a node valid for the client's lifetime) is added as a child of the root with the server ID as the name and latest transaction ID of its database as its content. For administrative purposes, a node called `master-notify` is created along with its watch. When more machines are added, they find the root and perform the same basic operations (apart from the administrative ones). Any node can read and write the content of any other node (the node in the cluster and not the one in the graph!).

So, the ephemeral node exists during the lifetime of an instance and is removed from the children of the root when the instance fails and a deletion event is sent to all other instances. If the failed instance was a master, then it will trigger an election and the result will be broadcast by a write to the `master-notify` node. A master election can also be triggered when a new instance is added to the cluster. Hence, the transaction ID must be up to date to avoid the current master from losing the election. Hence, the coordinator service needs to be configured and maintained. After this head start, you can now explore more of the HA source.

Summary

In this chapter, we took a peek into the working of Neo4j under the hood, though not in detail, but enough to give you a start to explore the source yourself. You learned how the core classes for storage, the caching mechanism, and the transactions, worked. We also explored the high availability cluster operations and the master election mechanism.

In the next chapter we will take a look at a few useful tools that are built for and around Neo4j to ease the life of users and admins and look into relevant use cases for the same.

7
Administering Neo4j

In the course of time that Neo4j has been around, it has become a widely accepted tool for storage and processing of large scale, highly interconnected data. From major corporations such as eBay and Walmart, to research students, the utilities of Neo4j have spread across the world. What makes Neo4j a great tool, is the fact that it is open source, and community contributions are useful and valuable. Today, Neo4j can be interfaced with several frameworks and a plethora of tools have been developed to make operations like data loading, traversals, and testing, simpler and more effective. It is not always about having an effective place for your application; it is also about maintaining and administering it to obtain optimum performance from the application. In this chapter, we will first look at how to use the Neo4j adapters for some of the most popular languages and frameworks that are used today. In the latter part of the chapter, we will see how admins can tweak and change the configurations of a standard Neo4j system, so that an optimum performance system can be obtained. The topics to be covered in this chapter can be summarized as follows:

- Interfacing Neo4j with PHP, JavaScript, and Python
- Configuring Neo4j Server, JVM, and caches
- Memory mapped I/O settings
- Logging configurations
- Security of Neo4j Server

Interfacing with the tools and frameworks

Neo4j as a core data storage solution is quite powerful but, with the increasing sophistication of use and rapid development practices, several tools were developed as an effort to increase the efficiency and compatibility of a Neo4j system. Adapters for various well known languages for server-side and client-side development have sprung up, making the development process for Neo4j based web applications simpler. Let us take a look at the use of some of the Neo4j adapters for the most common web platform technologies.

Using Neo4j for PHP developers

PHP is one of the most widely popular web development languages for creating dynamic content based application. Some common frameworks such as Wordpress and CakePHP are developed with PHP. Now, if you are trying to develop a PHP application, and want Neo4j at the backend for data storage and processing, you can use the Neo4jPHP adapter very well. It is written by Josh Adell, and it exposes an API that encourages intuitiveness and flexibility of use. Neo4jPH also incorporates some advantageous performance enhancements of its own, in the form of lazy-loading and caching. Let us take a look at some basic usage of this tool.

Use an editor to create a script and name it `connection_test.php`. Add the following lines to it:

```php
<?php
    require('vendor/autoload.php');

    $client = new Everyman\Neo4j\Client('localhost', 7474);
    print_r($client->getServerInfo());
```

If you have a database instance running on a different machine or port, you need to accordingly change `localhost` to the complete address of the database machine, and `7474` to the appropriate port number.

You can now execute the script from a server instance or in a standalone manner to view the result:

```
> php connection_test.php
```

If your server information displays successfully, then you have set up a basic Neo4jPHP code. You can view the source of the project at `https://github.com/jadell/neo4jphp` along with the detailed documentation at `https://github.com/jadell/neo4jphp/wiki/Introduction`.

The JavaScript Neo4j adapter

JavaScript is one of the most widely used client-side scripting languages. You can now communicate with your client-side application along with the Neo4j server with the use of the request module of the Node.js framework. Any other JavaScript module which can interact with the Neo4j server by sending and receiving queries can also be used. You can get a detailed description of the formats and protocols of the Neo4j REST API endpoints from the official documentation at `http://neo4j.com/docs/stable/rest-api-transactional.html`. You can also perform operations like sending multiple statements in a request, as well as sharing a transaction between several requests. The following basic function can be used to access the remote REST endpoint with the help of JavaScript:

```
var req=require("request");
var traxUrl = "http://localhost:7474/db/data/transaction/commit";
function cypher(query,params,cb) {
  req.post({uri:traxUrl,
        json:{statements:[{statement:query,parameters:params}]}},
        function(err,res) { cb(err,res.body)})
}
```

The `cypher()` function can send a cypher request from the JavaScript code to the Neo4j server and receive a response in JSON format. To use this function in your application, you can use the following format:

```
var query="MATCH (n:User) RETURN n, labels(n) as l LIMIT {limit}"
var params={limit: 10}
var cb=function(err,data) { console.log(JSON.stringify(data)) }

cypher(query,params,cb)

{"results":[
  {"columns":["n","l"],
    "data":[
      {"row":[{"name":"Aran"},["User"]]}
    ]
  }],
  "errors":[]}
```

The JSON form of the results is displayed upon execution. For applications built on top of the Node.js framework, you can use the Node.js-specific driver for Neo4j as well. You can learn more about it at `https://github.com/thingdom/node-neo4j`.

Neo4j with Python

Neo4j provides extensive support for Python and its web framework, Django. Py2neo is a simple library written by Nigel Small, providing access to the Neo4j REST API, and even supports Cypher queries. It has no external dependencies and is actively maintained on Github. You can follow the project at `https://github.com/nigelsmall/py2neo`.

For the Django framework, neo4django is an **Object Graph Mapper** (**OGM**) with which you can create the model definitions in Django, along with queries for Neo4j. It is also community supported and is useful for graph web applications running Django at the backend. The project can be found at `https://github.com/scholrly/neo4django`.

There are several other tools and frameworks to make the task of interfacing Python applications with Neo4j painless. The most popular ones are the BulbFlow framework (`http://bulbflow.com/`) which is an ORM for graph traversals using Gremlin at the backend. NeoModel (`https://github.com/robinedwards/neomodel`) is another tool with support for Django. However, a detailed discussion of these frameworks is beyond the scope of this book.

Admin tricks

A database is the life force behind an application, and that calls for a high degree of initial optimization depending upon the type and size of data to be stored and resources available on the server. Being written in Java, Neo4j also requires you to configure the Java related parameters properly as well. In the upcoming sections, we will look at how you can tweak your system and database configurations to maintain your Neo4j data store in good health.

Server configuration

For advanced usage of the Neo4j database, you can configure several parameters to keep the resources in check. The primary configuration file, Neo4j, is located in the `conf/neo4j-server.properties` directory. For normal development purposes, the default settings are sufficient. However, as an administrator, you can make suitable changes to the settings.

You can set the base directory on the disk where your database resides using the following property:

```
org.neo4j.server.database.location=/path/to/database/graph.db
```

The default port on which Neo4j operates is 7474. However, you can change the port for accessing the data, UI and administrative use, using the following setting:

```
org.neo4j.server.webserver.port=9098
```

You can even configure the client access pattern depending upon the address of the Neo4j database relative to the application that uses it. This helps in restricting the use of the database to the specific application. The default value is the loopback 127.0.0.1, which can be changed with:

```
#allowonly client's IP to connect
org.neo4j.server.webserver.address=192.168.0.2

#any client allowed to connect
org.neo4j.server.webserver.address=0.0.0.0
```

You can set the **rrdb (round robin database directory)** for collecting the metrics on the instance of database running. You can even specify to the database the URI path to be used for accessing the database with the REST API (it is a relative path and the default value is /db/data). The following settings are used:

```
org.neo4j.server.webadmin.rrdb.location=data/graph.db/../rrd

org.neo4j.server.webadmin.data.uri=/db/data/
```

The Neo4j WebAdmin interface uses a different relative path to provide access to the management tool. You can specify the URI setting as follows:

```
org.neo4j.server.webadmin.management.uri=/db/manage
```

If the Neo4j database resides on a separate machine in the network, you can restrict the class of network addresses that can access it (IPv4 or IPv6 or both). You need to modify the settings in the conf/neo4j-wrapper.conf file. Look for the section titled *Java Additional Parameters*, and append the following parameter to it:

```
wrapper.java.additional.3=-Djava.net.preferIPv4Stack=true
```

In order to configure the number of threads controlling the concurrency level in the servicing of the HTTP requests by the Neo4j server, you can use the following parameter:

```
org.neo4j.server.webserver.maxthreads=200
```

A timeout is used by the Neo4j server to manage orphaned or broken transactions. So, if no requests are received for an open transaction for a period configured in the timeout (the default is 60s), the transaction is rolled back by the server. You can configure it as:

```
org.neo4j.server.transaction.timeout=60
```

The main file for server configurations is conf/neo4j-server.properties. For parameters to tune the performance of the database at a low level, a second file called the neo4j.proprties file is used. You can explicitly set this file using the org.neo4j.server.db.tuning.properties=neo4j.properties parameter which, if not set, the server looks for in the current directory as the neo4j-server. properties file. If no file is present, then a warning is logged by the server. When the neo4j.properties file is set and the server is restarted, this file is loaded and the database engine is configured accordingly.

JVM configurations

Neo4j is written in Java and hence, the settings for JVM also decide the resource constraints that are imposed upon the database. You can however, configure these properties in the conf/neo4j-wrapper.conf file in NEO4J_HOME in your installation. Here are a few common properties that you can tweak according to your requirements:

Name of property	What it stands for
wrapper.java.initmemory	Initial size of heap (in MB)
wrapper.java.maxmemory	Maximum size of heap (in MB)
wrapper.java.additional.N	Additional literal parameter of the JVM (N is the number of each literal)

The underlying JVM has two parameters that are used to control the main memory – one each for the stack and the heap. In Neo4j, the heap size is a critical parameter, since it controls the allocation of objects (number of objects) by the database engine. The stack, on the other hand, is the deciding factor for the depth of the call stack for the application.

Generally, the notion is that having a large heap size is better. With a large heap, Neo4j can handle transactions that are much larger, and also experience high concurrency in transactions. Neo4j speed will also increase as a bigger section of the graph and will fit in the caches, leading to more frequently used nodes and relationships being quickly accessible. Also, with a larger heap, the nodes and relationship caches will be much larger as well.

However, as an admin, you need to make sure that the heap fits in the system's main memory, because if paging to disk occurs, then the performance is adversely affected. Also, if your heap size is much larger than the requirement of the application, then the JVM garbage collection leaves dead objects lying around for a longer time. This, in turn, will cause longer pauses for garbage collection, and latency issues which is not desired by the application. In a 32 bit JVM, the default heap size is 64 megabytes, which is too small for practical applications (a 64-bit JVM heap is not useful either). Memory is a critical factor when transactions are prominent in the system. The following figure shows the memory footprints of different transaction types:

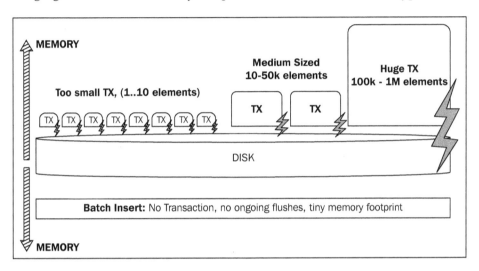

Depending on the cache implementation being used, a suitable heap size coupled with garbage collection can be used to handle most traffic by the database. The default soft reference cache (LRU based) needs a heap larger than the data to be kept in it, thereby being able to cache most nodes and relationships. It will let the heap get too full, then it will trigger a garbage collection which will result in loss of cached data. The cache storage can be prolonged by using a much larger cache. If a strong reference cache is being used, then the entire graph must fit in the heap (cache). Thus large heaps can avoid out-of-memory exceptions and maintain high overall throughput.

A weak reference cache, on the other hand, can be allocated heap, just enough for handling the peak load (average memory x peak load) and is beneficial in low latency scenarios.

Number of primitives	RAM size	Heap configuration	Reserved RAM for the OS
10M	2GB	512MB	The rest
100M	8GB+	1-4GB	1-2GB
1B+	16GB-32GB+	4GB+	1-2GB

Caches

Caches in Neo4j are of two basic types:

- **File buffer cache**: It is used to cache the storage file data as it is stored on the storage media
- **Object cache**: It is used for caching of nodes, relationships and properties to be used for speeding traversals, and transactions

The Neo4j data is stored in the file buffer cache in a format identical to that used for the representation of a persistent storage medium. This cache is helpful in improving the read/write performance by writing to cache, and delaying writing to the persistent storage till the rotation of the logical log. It is a safe operation since all stored files for the transaction can be recovered in case a crash occurs.

Let us take a look at how data is stored in Neo4j and the files used for storage onto the underlying file system. Each file in the Neo4j storage file stores uniform records of a fixed size and a specific type:

Store file	Record size	Contents
neostore.nodestore.db	15 B	Nodes
neostore.relationshipstore.db	34 B	Relationships
neostore.propertystore.db	41 B	Properties for nodes and relationships
neostore.propertystore.db.strings	128 B	Values of string properties
neostore.propertystore.db.arrays	128 B	Values of array properties

You can configure the size of the records during the creation of the data store with the help of the `array_block_size` and the `string_block_size` parameters. These settings come in handy when you expect to store large data records in the entities. Another advantage of these records is that you can estimate the storage requirements of the data in the graph, and calculate a rough cache size for the file buffer caches.

A file buffer cache exists for every distinct storage file. The file is divided by the cache into multiple equal-sized windows containing even numbers of records. In the process of caching, the windows that are most active are held in memory and the hit/miss ratio for each window is constantly tracked. When the ratio for a window that is uncached is found to be greater than those in the cache, one window from the cache is removed and is replaced by this window.

The object cache is used to cache nodes, relationships, and properties to optimize them for speedy graph traversals. Reading from the object cache experiences five to ten times the speed of accessing a file buffer cache. As soon as a node or relationship is accessed, it is added to the object cache. However, populations of the cached objects occur lazily. Loading of the properties only occur when the property is accessed. If a node is loaded into the cache, its relationships are not loaded until they are accessed.

You can configure the object cache using the `cache_type` parameter to specify the type of cache implementation to be used, mentioned separately for nodes and relationships. The available options for cache types are:

Cache type	Description
none	No high level cache is used. Object caching does not take place.
soft	Uses available memory optimally, and useful in high performing traversals. If cache size is inadequate for frequently used parts, garbage collector issues may occur. The community edition of Neo4j has this as the default cache type.
weak	It provides relatively short life spans for cached objects. For applications requiring high throughput, and where the frequently accessed section of the graph cannot fully fit into memory, this is a suitable solution.
strong	Best option for small completely in-memory graphs. This technique loads all data into memory without any removals or releases.
hpc	This refers to the high-performance cache. It dedicates memory chunks for caching nodes and relationships and is the best option in most scenarios. It facilitates fast lookups/writes and has a very small footprint. This cache type is available and is the default option for the Enterprise edition of Neo4j.

Apart from the `cache_type` parameter, there are a few other parameters that can be used to configure the way caches operate in Neo4j, and their resource constraints. Some of the important parameters are listed as follows:

Configuration option	Description (what it controls)	Example value
`cache.memory_ratio`	The percent of the available memory that will be used for caching. The default is 50 percent.	60.0
`node_cache_array_fraction`	The dedicated fraction of the heap size for the cache array for nodes (max ten).	8
`relationship_cache_array_fraction`	The dedicated fraction of the heap size for the cache array for relationships (max ten).	7
`node_cache_size`	The maximum amount of heap memory dedicated for caching nodes.	3G
`relationship_cache_size`	The maximum amount of the heap memory dedicated to caching relationships.	800M

Memory mapped I/O configuration

Memory mapped I/O can be used for read/writes to every file in the Neo4j storage. The best performance will be obtained if complete memory mapping of the file can occur, but if there is a shortage of memory for that, then Neo4j tries to optimize the memory use.

 Neo4j makes extensive use of the `java.nio` native Java package. Use of the native I/O package allows the allocation of memory external to the Java heap, which has to be handled separately. It will also depend on other system processes using memory. Neo4j allocates memory, which is a total of the JVM heap memory and the memory mapping needs, leaving the remaining memory for system processes.

It is not a great idea to use the complete available system memory for heap memory. The Neo4j data store (in the Neo4j database directory) stores the data in separate files which are outlined as follows:

- **nodestore**: It is used to store node information
- **relationshipstore**: It is used to store relationship information
- **propertystore**: All simple properties of nodes and relationships, occurring as primitive types are saved in this file
- **propertystore strings**: It is the storage for string type properties
- **propertystore arrays**: It is the storage of all array type properties

You can configure the memory mapping configurations for the mentioned files separately using the `mapped_memory` option along with the following parameters:

```
neostore.nodestore.db.mapped_memory=75M
neostore.relationshipstore.db.mapped_memory=100M
neostore.propertystore.db.mapped_memory=180M
neostore.propertystore.db.strings.mapped_memory=210M
neostore.propertystore.db.arrays.mapped_memory=210M
```

 If traversal speed is the highest priority, it is good to memory map the node and relationship stores as much as possible.

Traversal speed optimization example

Let us see an example that Neo4j uses to illustrate mapped memory allocation. In order to tune the settings for memory mapping, we need to first look up the size of the files in the data store in the Neo4j database directory. Let us take a case where the size of the files is found to be as follows:

```
neostore.nodestore.db: 14MB
neostore.propertystore.db: 510MB
neostore.propertystore.db.strings: 1.2GB
neostore.relationshipstore.db: 304MB
```

Let us say the system being used has a total memory of 4 GB, with 50 percent reserved for the system programs. The memory allocated to the Java Heap is 1.5 gigabytes leaving about 0.5 gigabytes for memory-mapping purposes. For obtaining optimum traversal speed, you can use a configuration for the memory mapping as follows:

```
neostore.nodestore.db.mapped_memory=15M
neostore.relationshipstore.db.mapped_memory=285M
neostore.propertystore.db.mapped_memory=100M
neostore.propertystore.db.strings.mapped_memory=100M
neostore.propertystore.db.arrays.mapped_memory=0M
```

Since our data had no file for array based properties, we can safely allocate no memory for memory mapping array based properties.

Batch insert example

Memory mapping can also be used to optimize batch insertion speed. Let us take a look at an example that Neo4j uses to demonstrate this. Suppose we have a graph with 10M nodes that are connected with 100M relationships. Every object has distinct primitive and string type properties. For simplicity, let's say there are no array based properties. We need to give more memory to the node and relationship stores. The allocations can be made as follows:

```
neostore.nodestore.db.mapped_memory=90M
neostore.relationshipstore.db.mapped_memory=3G
neostore.propertystore.db.mapped_memory=50M
neostore.propertystore.db.strings.mapped_memory=100M
neostore.propertystore.db.arrays.mapped_memory=0M
```

The configuration is intended to store the entire graph in memory. A naive way to calculate memory needed for mapping the nodes is by using the *number_of_nodes * 9 bytes* formula and, as for relationships, it can be *number_of_relationships * 33 bytes*. You will know why, if you have read about storage basics in the previous chapter. It is important to note that the above configuration requires a Java heap of more than 3.3G since, for batch inserter mode normal, Java buffers which are allocated on the JVM heap memory are used in place of memory mapped ones.

Neo4j server logging

The Neo4j server logs the information about the activities that takes place during the operating lifetime of the server. It is not an overhead; it is in fact an essential constituent for debugging, monitoring, and recovery. Neo4j provides support for logging of key server activity, HTTP request activity as well as garbage collection activity. Let us take a look at how to make use of these.

Server logging configurations

For event logging within the Neo4j server, the `java.util.logging` library of Java is used. You can configure the logging parameters in the `conf/logging.properties` file. The default level of logging is **INFO**, and the messages are printed on the terminal, as well as written to a rolling file located at `data/log`. Depending on the development stage and requirements, you can change the default behavior or even turn off the logging, using:

```
java.util.logging.ConsoleHandler.level=OFF
```

This will turn off all console output. The log files have a size limit of 10M after which rotation takes place. The files are named as `neo4j.<id>.<rotation sequence #>.log`. You can configure the naming scheme, frequency of rotation, and the size of the backlog using the following parameters respectively:

```
java.util.logging.FileHandler.pattern
java.util.logging.FileHandler.limit
java.util.logging.FileHandler.count
```

You can check out more about the `FileHandler` class of logging at `https://docs.oracle.com/javase/7/docs/api/java/util/logging/FileHandler.html`.

HTTP logging configurations

Along with events that occur within the Neo4j server, we can also log the HTTP requests and responses that are serviced by the Neo4j server. To achieve this, we need to configure the logger, location of logging, and the optimal format of the logs. You can enable HTTP logging by appending the following parameters defined in the `conf/neo4j-server.properties` file:

```
org.neo4j.server.http.log.enabled=true
org.neo4j.server.http.log.config=conf/neo4j-http-logging.xml
```

The first parameter indicates to the server that HTTP logging has been enabled for the server. You can toggle the behavior by setting the value to `false`. The second parameter specifies the format of logging, the file rollover settings that govern how the log output is formatted and stored. By default, an hourly log rotation is used and the generic common log format (http://en.wikipedia.org/wiki/Common_Log_Format).

If the log writes to a file, then the server initially checks whether the directory is existent with appropriate write permissions, failing which a failure is reported and the server does not start.

Garbage collection logging

We can also collect the logs from the garbage collector. In order to enable GC logging, we have to uncomment the following parameter so that the appropriate value is passed on to the server:

```
wrapper.java.additional.3=-Xloggc:data/log/neo4j-gc.log
```

GC logging cannot be directed to the terminal; we can find the log statements in `data/log/ne4j-gc.log`, or the appropriate directory that we had set in the preceding option value.

Logical logs

Logical logs are used as journals for the operations, and prove to be useful in scenarios when a recovery is needed for the database after a crash has occurred. The logs are generally rotated when the size exceeds a threshold (the default is 25M) and you can specify how many logs need to be kept. The reason for storing the logical log history is to serve incremental backups and keep the Neo4j HA clusters operational. When not enabled, the latest populated logical log is stored. We can configure the format using the following parameters:

```
keep_logical_logs=<true/false>
keep_logical_logs=<amount><type>
```

Some sample configurations can be specified as follows:

```
# To indefinitely keep logical logs
keep_logical_logs=true

# To store most recent populated log
keep_logical_logs=false

# To keep logical logs containing committed transactions for past 30
days.
```

```
keep_logical_logs=30 days

# To store logical logs that contain the most recent 500,000
transactions
keep_logical_logs=500k txs
```

The type option supports a few other cases which are listed as follows:

Type	Description	Example
files	Number of recent logical logs to persist	25 files
size	Maximum disk size that log files can occupy	250M size
txs	Number of most recent transactions to log	10M txs
hours	Store logs of committed transactions from past N hours from now.	12 hours
days	Store logs of committed transactions in past N days from now.	30 days

Open file size limit on Linux

When working with Neo4j, you need several files to be read in a concurrent manner, since the different entities are stored in different files. However, Linux platforms generally define an upper bound on the number of files that can be concurrently opened. You can check the limit for the current system user with:

```
user@localhost:~$ ulimit -n
1024
```

The default value (1024) is inadequate for most practical scenarios involving indexed entities or multiple server connections. You can increase this limit to a higher value. Generally, a value over 40000 is recommended, depending on the patterns of use. For the current session, you can change this value using the ulimit command, logging in as the root user for the system. To make a system-wide persistent effect, you need to follow these steps:

1. Open a terminal and log in as the root user using the following command:

   ```
   user@localhost:~$ sudo su -
   ```

2. When your prompt changes to root@localhost:~# you can use a text editor like vim or nano to open the /etc/security/limits.conf file.

3. Add the following lines to the file:

```
neo4j    soft    nofile   40000
neo4j    hard    nofile   40000
```

4. Open the `sudoers` file at `/etc/pam.d/su` and add/uncomment the following line

```
session    required    pam_limits.so
```

5. Restart your system to let the changes take effect.

In the preceding steps replace `neo4j` with the name of your current user. If you still see exceptions such as `Too many open files` or `Could not stat()` directory then the limit needs to be increased even further.

Neo4j server security

So, till now we looked at how to configure a Neo4j server in order to obtain optimum performance. However, in a practical scenario, we also need to ensure that our database server is secure enough to handle confidential and critical data. In this section, we will look at some aspects of securing the Neo4j database server.

Port and remote connection security

When a Neo4j server is started, the default behavior is to bind the host to the localhost with the connection port as 7474. Hence only local requests from the same machine are serviced. You can configure this behavior in the `conf/neo4j-server.properties` file by uncommenting, adding, or modifying the following lines:

```
# http port (for all data, administrative, and UI access)
org.neo4j.server.webserver.port=7474

#let the webserver only listen on the specified IP. Default
#is localhost (only accept local connections). Uncomment to allow
#any connection.
#org.neo4j.server.webserver.address=0.0.0.0
```

You can also restrict access to the database from only the machines(s) on which the application resides. So, only requests from this machine will be serviced. You can also provide open access (a security nightmare) by changing the incoming address to `0.0.0.0`. The following setting is used for this:

```
org.neo4j.server.webserver.address=0.0.0.0
```

Support for HTTPS

There is built-in support for encrypted communication with SSL over HTTPS in a Neo4j server installation. A private key and a self-signed SSL certificate is generated when the server is initiated. In production scenarios, self-signed certificates are not reliable. Hence, you can configure your own certificates and keys. You can either replace the generated key and certificate with your own, or modify the `conf/neo4j-server.properties` file to change the location of the key and certificates:

```
# Certificate location (auto generated if the file does not exist)
org.neo4j.server.webserver.https.cert.location=ssl/myapp.cert

# Private key location (auto generated if the file does not exist)
org.neo4j.server.webserver.https.key.location=ssl/myapp.key
```

You need to ensure that the key is encrypted and has the appropriate file permissions to enable read/write access for the server. There is also support for chained SSL certificates, where the certificates need to be merged in a single PEM file with the private key assuming the **DER** format. The option to enable/disable HTTPS support and define the port can be configured with these options:

```
# Support toggle for https: on/off
org.neo4j.server.webserver.https.enabled=true

# Port for https (for all data, administrative, and UI access)
org.neo4j.server.webserver.https.port=443
```

Server authorization rules

Apart from restrictions at the IP level, more detailed security policies may be required for administrators. The authorization policies for the Neo4j server controls access to database aspects on the basis of user or application credentials. The security rules must first be registered with the server, making scenarios for external lookup and authentication on the basis of role possible. The detailed configuration for this is managed in the `org.neo4j.server.rest.security.SecurityRule` package.

Setup server authorization rules enforcement

Let us look at a scenario in which a security rule for failure is being registered for restriction of access to all the external URIs. This can be configured in the `conf/neo4j-server.properties` file:

```
org.neo4j.server.rest.security_rules=rule.
CompleteRestrictionSecurityRule
```

The code for the `CompleteRestrictionSecurityRule` class can be defined in the following manner:

```
publicclassCompleteRestrictionSecurityRuleimplementsSecurityRule
{

publicstaticfinalStringMYREALM="MyApplication";

@Override
publicbooleanisAuthorized( HttpServletRequestrequest )
    {
returnfalse; // Forces failure always
// Logic for authorization coded here
    }

@Override
publicStringforUriPath()
    {
return"/*"; //For any incoming URI path
    }

@Override
publicStringwwwAuthenticateHeader()
    {
returnSecurityFilter.basicAuthenticationResponse(MYREALM);
    }
}
```

This rule restricts all types of access to the server from external locations. For a production scenario, you can configure the rule class to check for login credentials in order to authorize users to the application.

Sample request

```
POST http://localhost:7474/db/data/relationship/1
Accept:application/json; charset=UTF-8
```

Sample response

```
401:Unauthorized
WWW-Authenticate:Basic realm="MyApplication"
```

Security rules targeting with wildcards

Unlike the previous case, where all incoming requests are blocked, we can also target the restriction to some specific type of URIs with the use of wildcards. We need to register for this with a predefined wildcard URI path, with * specifying any section of the path. For example, /users* will block those requests that access the user root. In a similar fashion, the /users*type* expression refers to URIs accessing the type option for users like /users/mark/type/new.

You can use the defined CompleteRestrictionSecurityRule security rule class with a modification to the forUriPath method as follows:

```
publicStringforUriPath()
{
return"/secure/*";
}
```

This rule restricts only those requests that attempt to access the data under the /secure/ directory. So, with wildcards, you can flexibly control access to different parts of the server API.

Sample request

```
GET http://localhost:7474/secure/any/path/after/this/stuff
Accept:application/json; charset=UTF-8
```

Sample response

```
401:Unauthorized
WWW-Authenticate:Basic realm="MyApplication"
```

You can use multiple or a chain of wildcards in order to restrict a specific URI type or a pattern of URIs. Consider the case when the forUriPath() method is changed to take this form:

```
publicStringforUriPath()
    {
return"/protected/*/something/else/*/final/bit";
    }
```

The type of requests that this blocks are very specific and targeted in nature. An example of the type of request restricted is as follows:

Sample request

```
GET http://localhost:7474/protected/any/x/y/z/path/something/else/any/
subpath/final/bit/anything
Accept:application/json; charset=UTF-8
```

Example response

```
401:Unauthorized
WWW-Authenticate:Basic realm="MyApplication"
```

 As a default behavior, the Neo4j server allows functionality for remote scripting, thereby allowing complete access to the underlying database instance from anywhere. This is better for development purposes. However, in production stages, allowing remote scripting is a potential high security risk, and you need to impose a sound security layer.

Other security options

Apart from the numerous security configurations discussed, for critical deployments it is wise to use an additional proxy similar to Apache's mod_proxy (http://httpd. apache.org/docs/2.2/mod/mod_proxy.html). This can provide access control to specific IPs, a range of IPs and even URI patterns. So you can essentially allow /db/ data available to external clients while /db/admin/ can be made accessible from a specific IP. The configuration would look something like this:

```
<Proxy *>
   Order Deny,Allow
   Deny from all
   Allow from 192.168.0
</Proxy>
```

The proxy server gives the same functionality as Neo4j's default **SecurityRule** feature and you can also use both together with proper non-conflicting configurations. However, admins often prefer Apache to the default Neo4j feature.

Summary

In this chapter, we first looked at the utilities and adapters that have been developed for use with most popular languages and frameworks with Neo4j. We also looked into the configurations and tricks that administrators can make use of in order to obtain optimum performance out of their deployments. In the process, we also discussed caches, memory mapped I/O and logging configurations, and how we can secure access to a Neo4j server instance.

In the next chapter, we will be looking at a use case of Neo4j, where we will work on a recommendation engine, and discuss the best practices for development and deployment of a practical application.

8
Use Case – Similarity-based Recommendation System

In the previous chapters, we have studied about how to work with different aspects of the incredible graph database, Neo4j, from its installation, querying, and traversals, to performance optimizations at the production level. We have also had a peek under the hood of Neo4j in order to understand its functionality. Neo4j has a wide range of practical applications. Typically, any scenario that includes connected data represented graphically, Neo4j proves to be the perfect resource for storage and processing needs. With rapidly increasing connected devices and sensor driven technology, graph-based analytics solutions are becoming more popular in the business world, especially because they are simpler to interpret and visualize. Graph databases like Neo4j find extensive use in the route generation, fraud analysis, and impact analysis in networks. However, the latest and most popular use case of graph technologies is in the realm of recommendations. The booming sectors like social networks, job portfolio websites, and e-commerce solutions all operate with a sound recommendation engine at the backend. In this chapter let us understand how we can use Neo4j to address the issues in recommendation engines. The following topics will be discussed:

- Recommendation engine basics
- Building a recommendation engine
- Addressing map recommendation issues and visualization

The why and how of recommendations

In the consumer specific markets today, businesses need to stay a step ahead of the customer in order to flourish. Recommendations use the data that the customers generate, so that you can analyze patterns and behavior that can be used to suggest products, people, or point of sales. Over the years, several techniques have been developed to generate recommendations. Let us take a look at the major approaches:

Collaborative filtering

It is one of the most common techniques that recommendation engines today are based on. Collaborative Filtering refers to the method of pattern or information filtering with collaboration between various data sources, viewpoints, agents, etc. It uses previous or historical data of a user, or other users, to profile a pattern, and then uses it to predict what other content the user might like.

Let us take an example to understand this. On e-commerce websites, you are presented with suggestions for products that you might buy, based on the search history of your and other's profiles. Basically, based on the common data between you and other users, the websites can suggest products which the other people have browsed, but you haven't, yet. A similar scenario is applicable for social networks or dating websites. As an end user, when you have followed, befriended or expressed an interest in some people you would like to date, a system using collaborative filtering can give you suggestions for people who match your taste. The priority of the suggested results will depend upon what the results have in common with you, and what their tastes are.

In this way, the activities of other users is analyzed by the recommender system, thereby saving you precious time of browsing through profiles of irrelevant people. This is an extremely powerful system as it lets you benefit from the activities of people that you do not know or have never met. Thus collaborative filtering gives you a way to obtain concrete insights for applications that generate large sets of data.

Content-based filtering

Content-based filtering uses items or target descriptions along with the profile of the user's preferences. In such a system, each item is described and associated with certain keywords, and for each user, profiling is done for what the user likes. So the recommender system suggests items depending upon the user's own historical activities in order to recommend the items that best match.

Content-based filtering also uses weight values to signify how important the feature is for a particular user, and are calculated from the content rated by the user. User feedback, usually with likes, votes, or ratings, decide how important an attribute is for that user. An issue that content based recommendation faces, is being able to recommend content of multiple types based on patterns obtained from other types. For example, it is an easy task to recommend news based on the news browsing patterns of the user. However, it is a challenge to recommend products, forums, videos or music, based on the news browsing patterns. **Pandora Radio** is an excellent example of content based recommender, which uses the initial song of the user to find songs with similar characteristics.

The hybrid approach

We have seen the collaborative and content-based filtering methods, but research suggests that a hybrid of the two methods proves to be more effective. One way of generating hybrid results is to first separately get the results from the two methods and then combine them. You can also create a single model incorporating both techniques. Studies suggest that performance of the hybrid recommender systems is empirically better than that of the pure systems, and is known to give more accurate recommendations.

Netflix, the media content delivery website, is an excellent example of a hybrid system user. It compares the searching and viewing patterns of similar users and also provides results for movies that have some common characteristics of the users' high rated contents.

Let us take a look at some of the different techniques in which a hybrid system can be generated and used:

- **Switching**: This technique selects one or some of the recommendation components and applies it

- **Weighted**: In this technique, the numerical scores of the recommendation **components** are combined

- **Mixed**: Here, multiple recommendation systems operate together and the results from them are combined together

- **Augmentation of features**: A method is initially used to generate the feature set to be used and this set is then passed on the next method for providing recommendations

- **Combination of features**: A single recommendation system uses features from multiple different sources to generate results.

- **Cascading**: It is a priority based technique in which different recommendation systems have different priorities, which are used to settle ties in results

Building a recommendation system

Let us see how we can use Neo4j as the backbone to develop recommendation systems for different data scenarios. For this purpose, we will be using the collaborative filtering approach to process the data in hand and churn out relevant results.

In order to understand how the process works, let us use a simple data set of a dating site where you can sign in and view the profile of people who you could potentially date, and you can follow or like them, or vice versa. The graphical representation of such a dataset will represent the people as nodes, and the like operations from one person to another is represented as edges between them.

As shown in the following diagram, consider a user, John, who has just registered on the website and created a profile for himself. He begins browsing through profiles of women, searching for a person that might interest him. After going through the profiles of several people, he likes the profiles of three of them – Donna, Rose, and Martha. Now, as John is trying his luck, there are other users on the site who are also actively searching. It turns out that Jack, Rory, Sean, and Harry have also liked profiles of some of the people that John has liked. So, it can be inferred that their tastes are aligned and similar. So, it is quite probable that John might like some of the other people that the guys have already liked, but whose profiles John has yet to come across. This is where the collaborative filtering comes into play, and we can suggest more options for John to view, so that he has to deal with a lesser number of irrelevant profiles.

The following diagram is an illustration of what type of relationships from our dataset are being used by the recommender:

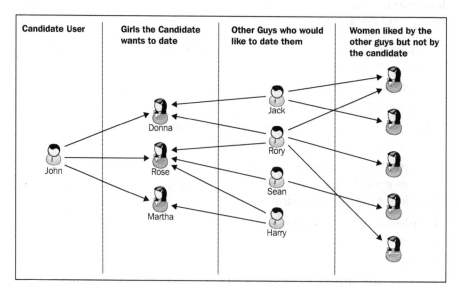

Creating this type of a system would require complex search and set operations for a production-level implementation. This is where Neo4j comes to the rescue. What we are essentially doing in the technique above, is searching for some desired patterns in the graphical representation of our data, and analyzing the results of each sub-search to obtain a final result set. This reminds us of a Neo4j specific tool we have studied before – Cypher. It is beneficial to use Cypher in recommender systems, because of the following reasons:

- It works on the principal of pattern matching, and therefore is perfect for implementing collaborative recommendation algorithms.

- Cypher, being a declarative query language, does not need you to write code for how to match the query patterns. You will simple need to mention what to match and get results. This leads to simpler and smaller codes for creating complex recommendation systems.

- Cypher, designed specifically for Neo4j will give optimum performance for relatively large datasets, compared to writing native code for generating recommendations.

The following code segment illustrates how the scenario described above can be represented using Cypher.

```
START Person = node(2)
MATCH Person-[IS_INTERESTED_BY]->someone<-[:IS_INTERESTED_BY]-
otherguy-[:IS_INTERESTED_BY]->recommendations
WHERE not(Person = otherguy)
RETURN count(*) AS PriorityWeight, recommendations.name AS name
ORDER BY PriorityWeight DESC, name DESC;
```

Let us see what different parts of the preceding Cypher segment are doing in the overall scenario:

1. We initially select the user who is the candidate for the recommendations using the following query:

   ```
   START Person = node(2)
   ```

2. The main pattern that we are searching for is about finding the women that are liked by the people who co-incidentally share common likes with our recommendation candidate. The following query illustrates it:

   ```
   MATCH Person-[IS_INTERESTED_BY]->someone<-[:IS_INTERESTED_BY]-
   otherguy-[:IS_INTERESTED_BY]->recommendations
   ```

3. We rule out the consideration of our candidate as a tertiary user, since by default, the candidate, John, shares the same likes as himself which would result in a redundant case. Hence the following statement:

```
WHERE not(Paul = otherguy)
```

4. Using the `count` method, we monitor the number of ways a result is obtained during the query execution, using the following statement:

```
RETURN count(*) AS PriorityWeight, recommendations.name AS name
```

5. Finally, we return the results in the order of relevance (using the sort method for ordering):

```
ORDER BY PriorityWeight DESC, name DESC;
```

Let us take an example of another social dataset to understand a more complex pattern for recommending people to date. This dataset (`social2.db` in the code for this chapter) contains names of people along with their genders, dating orientations, attributes/qualities the person has, where they live, and the qualities they a looking for in potential partner.

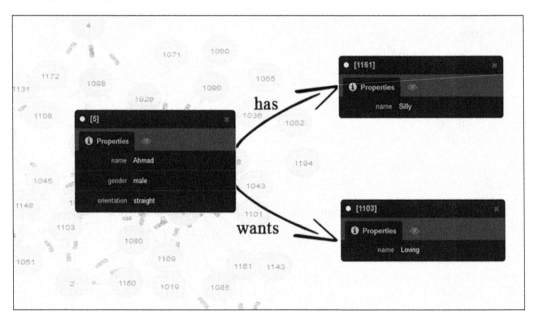

So, let us build upon the recommendation algorithm, one step at a time:

1. First, we need the name of the person who is looking for a person to date. The following statement can be used if you know the name:

    ```
    START me=node:users_index(name = 'Albert')
    ```

2. In order to provide recommendations, we need to consider people living in a nearby location or same town, since a person from Alaska will not prefer to date someone from California (you know how long distance dates turn out!!). So the following statement can be used to filter:

    ```
    MATCH me-[:lives_in]->city<-[:lives_in]-person
    ```

3. From the results obtained in the preceding step, we need to match the genders of the prospective person with the candidate depending upon his/her orientation.

4. We also need to match the qualities that our candidate is looking for and the qualities that the prospective person possesses. We can't be selfish though!

5. We also check if the candidate possesses the qualities that the prospective person is looking for. Hence, the following statement follows:

    ```
    WHERE me.orientation = person.orientation AND
        ((me.gender <> person.gender AND me.orientation = "straight"))
    AND
        me-[:wants]->()<-[:has]-person AND
        me-[:has]->()<-[:wants]-person
    WITH DISTINCT city.name AS city_name, person, me
    MATCH   me-[:wants]->attributes<-[:has]-person-[:wants]-
    >requirements<-[:has]-me
    ```

6. To check the results obtained at this stage, you can collect the results from the preceding statement, process them to find the number of matching attributes between the candidate and the prospective person, by using the following statement:

    ```
    RETURN city_name, person.name AS person_name,
        COLLECT(attributes.name) AS my_interests,
        COLLECT(requirements.name) AS their_interests,
        COUNT(attributes) AS matching_wants,
        COUNT(requirements) AS matching_has
    ```

7. Depending on the practical utility of the application for which the recommender operates, you can even sort the results on the basis of relevance, and display to the candidate the top results.

    ```
    ORDER BY (COUNT(attributes)/(1.0 / COUNT(requirements)))) DESC
    LIMIT 10
    ```

Hence, the overall Cypher query for this recommendation algorithm will look like the following:

```
START me=node:users_index(name = 'Albert')
MATCH me-[:lives_in]->city<-[:lives_in]-person
WHERE me.orientation = person.orientation AND
    ((me.gender <> person.gender AND me.orientation = "straight")) AND
      me-[:wants]->()<-[:has]-person AND
      me-[:has]->()<-[:wants]-person
WITH DISTINCT city.name AS city_name, person, me
MATCH  me-[:wants]->attributes<-[:has]-person-[:wants]->requirements<-
[:has]-me
RETURN city_name, person.name AS person_name,
       COLLECT(attributes.name) AS my_interests,
       COLLECT(requirements.name) AS their_interests,
       COUNT(attributes) AS matching_wants,
       COUNT(requirements) AS matching_has
ORDER BY (COUNT(attributes)/(1.0 / COUNT(requirements))) DESC
LIMIT 10
```

If you start Neo4j with the `social2.db` dataset provided in the code for this chapter, you will find that the preceding query generates the following results view in the web interface:

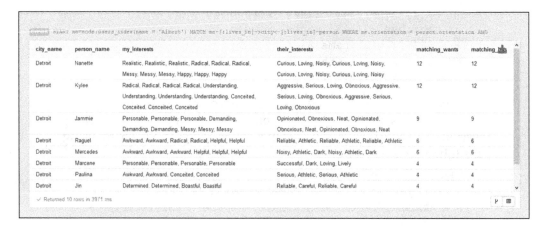

Thus, the results are displayed in tabular format containing the people with the most matching traits with our candidate. You can also export these results from the interface to be used in a tertiary part of your web application.

The preceding algorithm is a simple representation of a recommendation system. Much more complex systems can be constructed by combining multiple such clauses together. Of course, similar operations can be performed with map data as well, for recommendations of places to visit, or with sales data for providing suggestions to customers for products they are likely to buy. However, all this is possible in a minimalistic approach with the help of graph based technologies like Neo4j and Cypher.

Recommendations on map data

Map data is more complex and critical than sales or social data. However, its one advantage over the others, is that it is mostly static in nature. So what kind of recommendations can we generate for map data? Suppose a user searches for a location on the map, you can generate suggestions for nearby places of interest depending upon the user's search history. For example, if a user searches for restaurants once in a while, you could generate suggestions for restaurants in any new locations that he visits. Let us look at how to approach this issue.

Consider a map data set which represents the locations in the form of nodes, and the roads connecting them in the form of bi-directional relationships. The **Location** entity and its properties can be illustrated as follows

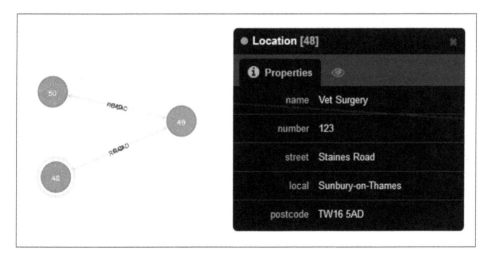

The **Road** entity and its property structure can be illustrated in the web interface as follows:

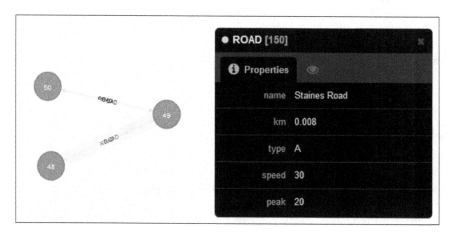

So, the map graph by itself is not sufficient to create a recommendation system. We will need to add it to scenarios involving user specific data, such as location based searches (advertisements or establishments to be recommended based on location and proximity of the user) or favorable logistic paths (delivery of goods through cab services is a very good example, where a cabbie can deliver goods to a location if he is already headed that way. Hence, a recommender system can be devised to suggest delivery locations to cabbies based on the areas they frequent or routes they take. The possibilities are endless when you can reference a map graph from a social or transport graph. So you combine the social graph and the map graph given above, by linking a person from the first to his corresponding locality in the second. This dual layered graph will now allow you to operate on the map, when you are simultaneously traversing the social graph.

A similar approach can be taken for airlines or logistic graphs, where the map component of the graph and the chief operation can be logically segregated, but physically linked. Now you can devise your own recommendation algorithms to consider location info for generating suggestions. Since you have now used pattern matching to generate recommendations for social data, we leave for you an exercise to devise a recommender for maps, according to any of the scenarios discussed earlier.

Visualization of graphs

Recommendations not only help the end user or consumer, but are a boon for analysts and business managers as well. Using graph databases like Neo4j to create such systems also brings the added advantage of great visualization support through its own web interface as well as several third party tools. Visualization serves two basic purposes which are outlined as follows:

- Better understanding of the data and the level of connectivity of the data makes it easier to plan the development process

- Analysts can use visualizations to suggest improvements to the result generation process since a visual outlook gives a better perspective

If we consider the example of the dating application earlier, a visual overview can assist in the identification of anomalies or outlier entities. For example, if a person is a trouble seeker and likes to spam other people's profiles, it would show up in the majority of connections being singular. Such cases can be identified and protected against, by using proper visualization method.

There are several tools available that help to visualize graph data. The web interface of Neo4j comes with its own visualization tool, where the results are displayed in the form of a fluid graph interface with dynamic functionality to view the information about specific displayed entities. This is how our complete map graph is visualized in the web interface of Neo4j:

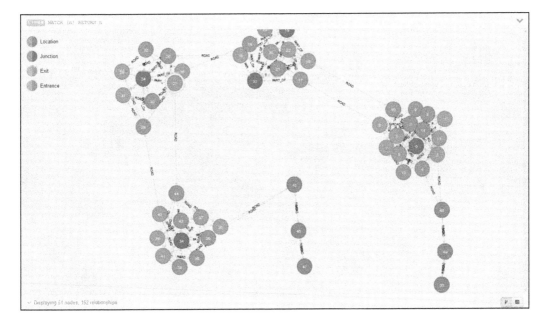

The **gephi** open source project is also an excellent tool to visualize complex and dynamic graphs. It is a great tool for data analysis and inference and can support a large number of graph sources. However, **Linkurious** is a project that deserves special mention as it is built with Neo4j in mind. It is a versatile tool, which provides a frontend to most of the graph database operations. Not only does it allow you to visualize and explore the database, it also provides a search functionality to search your graph data without any code (like a Google for graphs). You can even edit entities in the graph from the Linkurious frontend.

 You can learn more about the project at https://linkurio.us/. If you are an admin, you will love to work with this.

Here's what the interface looks like:

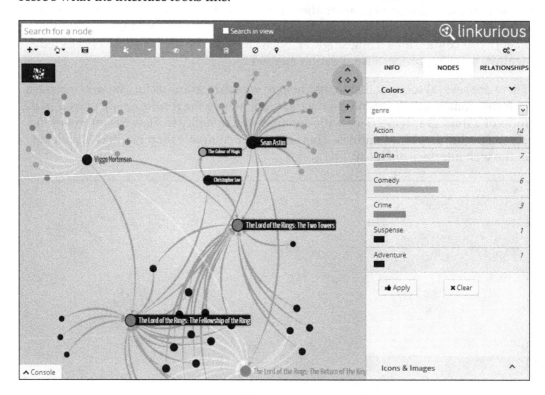

Summary

In this chapter, we have seen how Neo4j, as a graph database, is the best available option for creating recommendation systems based on similarity. This takes advantage of the pattern matching nature of the Cypher query language. We also looked at a social network recommender example, and also discussed how to incorporate map data into the generated suggestions. Finally, we saw the importance of data visualization and the major tools available for this objective. Thus, this book not only brings to you the in-depth study and administration of the Neo4j database, but also leaves you with one of the critical and widely popular use cases in the industry today.

Index

L

Least Recently Used (LRU) 126
LinkBench
  about 110
  URL 110
Linkurious
  about 168
  URL 168
LockManager 131, 132
LogEntry state 129
logical logs 150

M

manual indexing 50, 51
map data
  about 165
  recommendations 165, 166
MATCH clause 41
Maven
  about 100
  URL 25
MemcacheDB 11
memory mapped I/O configuration
  about 146
  batch insert example 148
  configuring 147
  nodestore 147
  propertystore 147
  propertystore arrays 147
  propertystore strings 147
  relationshipstore 147
  traversal speed optimization example 147
MERGE clause 42
migration techniques, for SQL users
  about 54
  data sync 57
  dual data stores, handling 54
  initial import 56
  model, analyzing 54, 55
  result 57
MongoDB 13

N

Neo4j
  about 14
  administering 137
  characteristics 18
  cloud deployment, with Azure 31-35
  configuring, for Amazon clusters 29, 30
  CRUD operations 20, 21
  design constraints 64
  download link 22
  for high-volume applications 79
  graphs 8
  indexing 50
  interfacing, with frameworks 138
  interfacing, with Python 140
  interfacing, with tools 138
  processing engine 18
  server, unit testing 106
  storage file 144, 145
  storage within 18
  using, for PHP developers 138
Neo4j applications
  benchmarking performance,
    with Gatling 110-112
  performance testing 107-110
  scaling 112-115
  testing 100
  unit testing 101
Neo4j configurations
  about 21
  embedded mode 22-26
  server mode 26, 27
Neo4j Enterprise
  URL 27
Neo4j graph database
  about 16
  ACID compliance 17
  characteristics 19
Neo4j HA
  about 112
  cache sharding 113
  issues 113
  neo4j-01.local 27

Thank you for buying
Neo4j High Performance

About Packt Publishing

Packt, pronounced 'packed', published its first book, *Mastering phpMyAdmin for Effective MySQL Management*, in April 2004, and subsequently continued to specialize in publishing highly focused books on specific technologies and solutions.

Our books and publications share the experiences of your fellow IT professionals in adapting and customizing today's systems, applications, and frameworks. Our solution-based books give you the knowledge and power to customize the software and technologies you're using to get the job done. Packt books are more specific and less general than the IT books you have seen in the past. Our unique business model allows us to bring you more focused information, giving you more of what you need to know, and less of what you don't.

Packt is a modern yet unique publishing company that focuses on producing quality, cutting-edge books for communities of developers, administrators, and newbies alike. For more information, please visit our website at www.packtpub.com.

About Packt Open Source

In 2010, Packt launched two new brands, Packt Open Source and Packt Enterprise, in order to continue its focus on specialization. This book is part of the Packt Open Source brand, home to books published on software built around open source licenses, and offering information to anybody from advanced developers to budding web designers. The Open Source brand also runs Packt's Open Source Royalty Scheme, by which Packt gives a royalty to each open source project about whose software a book is sold.

Writing for Packt

We welcome all inquiries from people who are interested in authoring. Book proposals should be sent to author@packtpub.com. If your book idea is still at an early stage and you would like to discuss it first before writing a formal book proposal, then please contact us; one of our commissioning editors will get in touch with you.

We're not just looking for published authors; if you have strong technical skills but no writing experience, our experienced editors can help you develop a writing career, or simply get some additional reward for your expertise.

Learning Neo4j

ISBN: 978-1-84951-716-4   Paperback: 222 pages

Run blazingly fast queries on complex graph datasets with the power of the Neo4j graph database

1. Get acquainted with graph database systems and apply them in real-world use cases.

2. Get started with Neo4j, a unique NOSQL database system that focuses on tackling data complexity.

3. A practical guide filled with sample queries, installation procedures, and useful pointers to other information sources.

Learning Cypher

ISBN: 978-1-78328-775-8   Paperback: 162 pages

Write powerful and efficient queries for Neo4j with Cypher, its official query language

1. Improve performance and robustness when you create, query, and maintain your graph database.

2. Save time by writing powerful queries using pattern matching.

3. Step-by-step instructions and practical examples to help you create a Neo4j graph database using Cypher.

Please check **www.PacktPub.com** for information on our titles

Instant OpenCV for iOS

ISBN: 978-1-78216-384-8   Paperback: 96 pages

Learn how to build real-time computer vision applications for the iOS platform using the OpenCV library

1. Learn something new in an Instant! A short, fast, focused guide delivering immediate results.

2. Build and run your OpenCV code on iOS.

3. Become familiar with iOS fundamentals and make your application interact with the GUI, camera, and gallery.

4. Build your library of computer vision effects, including photo and video filters.

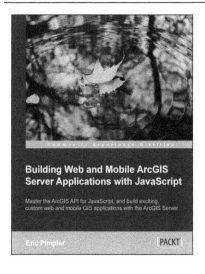

Building Web and Mobile ArcGIS Server Applications with JavaScript

ISBN: 978-1-84969-796-5   Paperback: 274 pages

Master the ArcGIS API for JavaScript, and build exciting, custom web and mobile GIS applications with the ArcGIS Server

1. Develop ArcGIS Server applications with JavaScript, both for traditional web browsers as well as the mobile platform.

2. Acquire in-demand GIS skills sought by many employers.

3. Step-by-step instructions, examples, and hands-on practice designed to help you learn the key features and design considerations for building custom ArcGIS Server applications.

Please check **www.PacktPub.com** for information on our titles